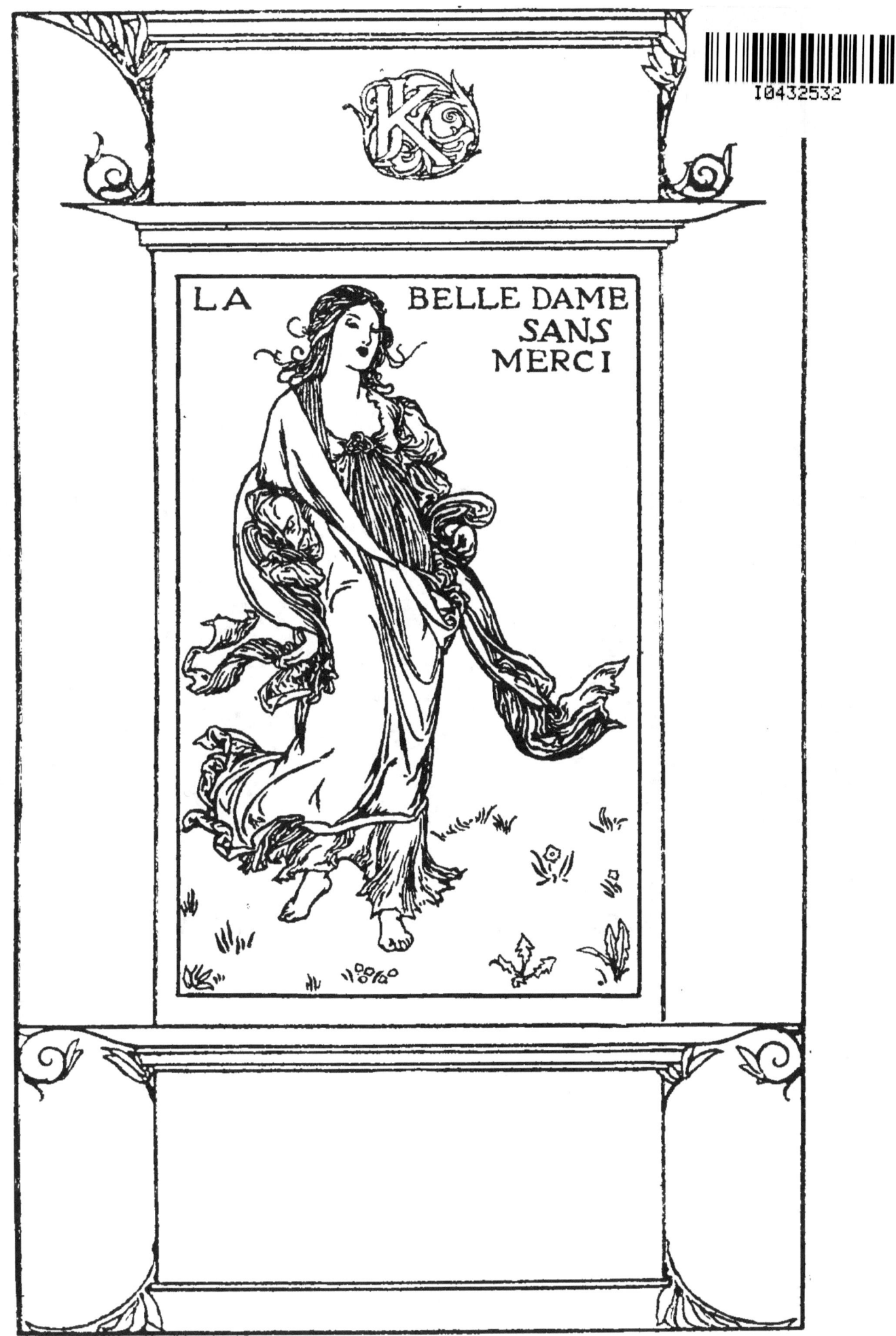

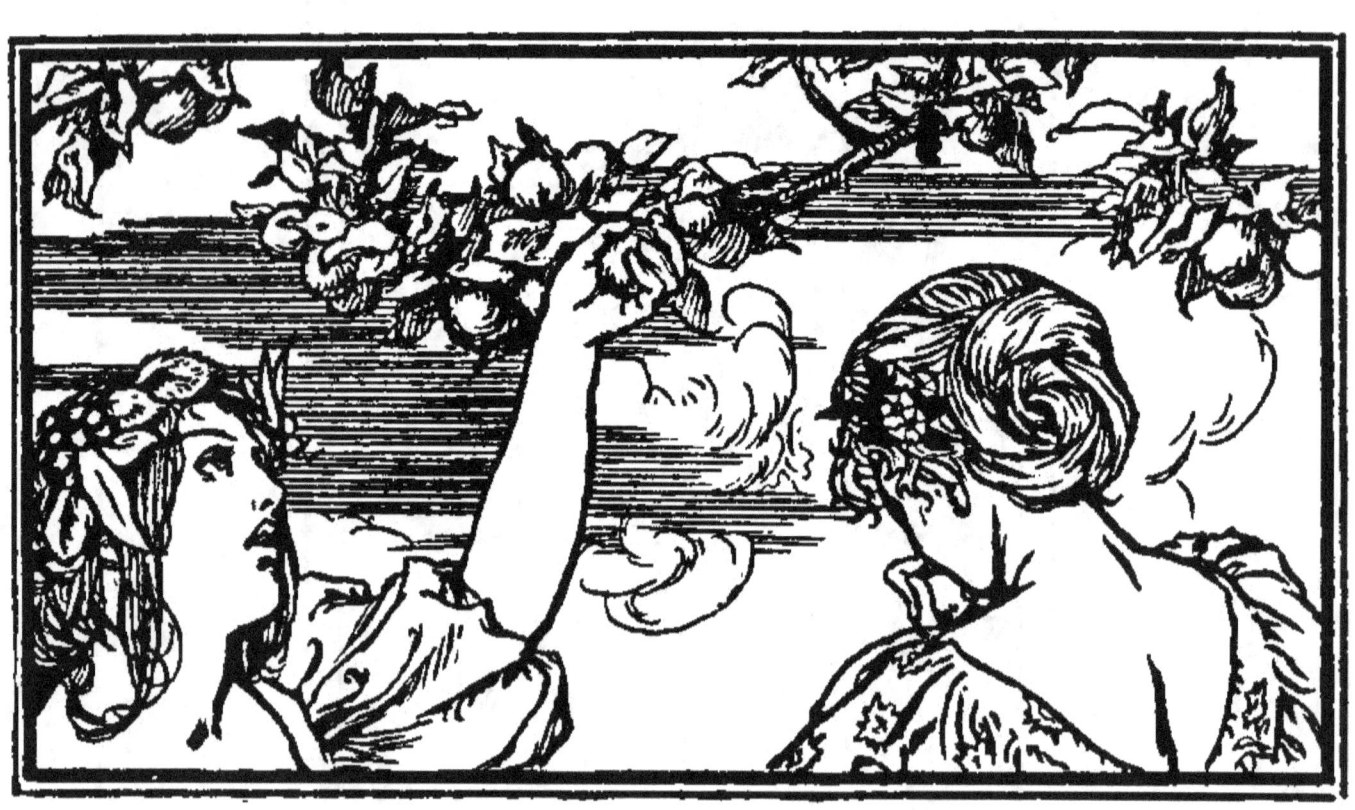

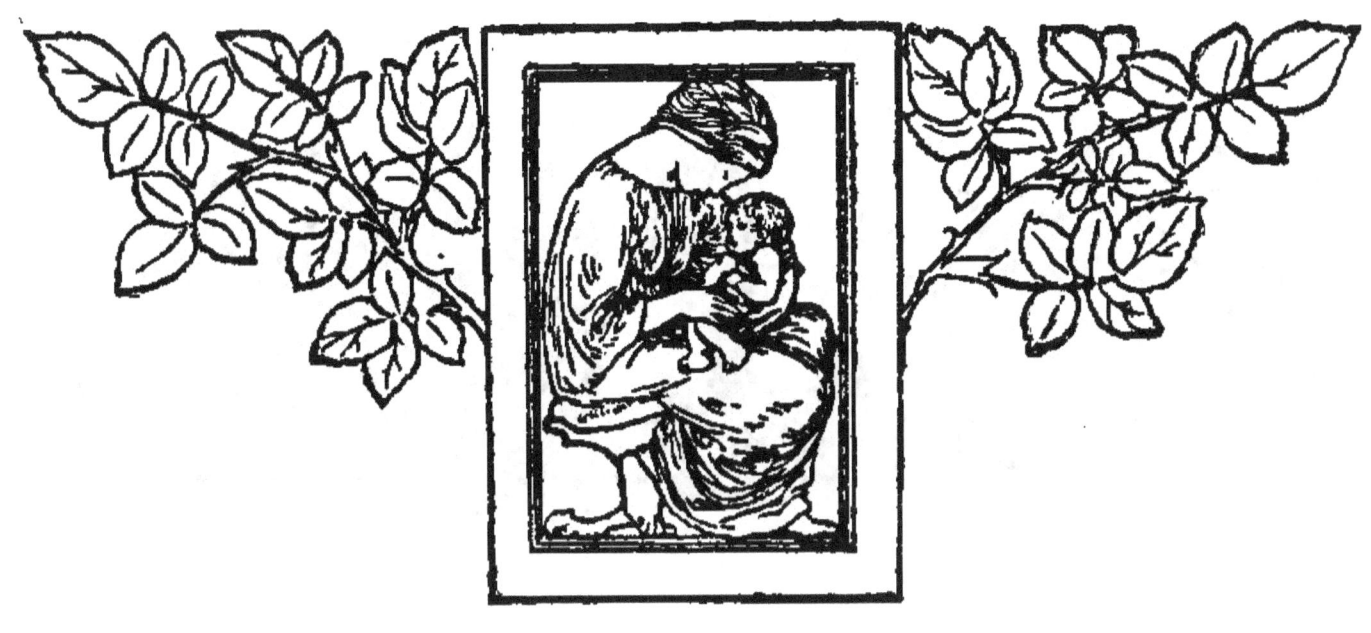

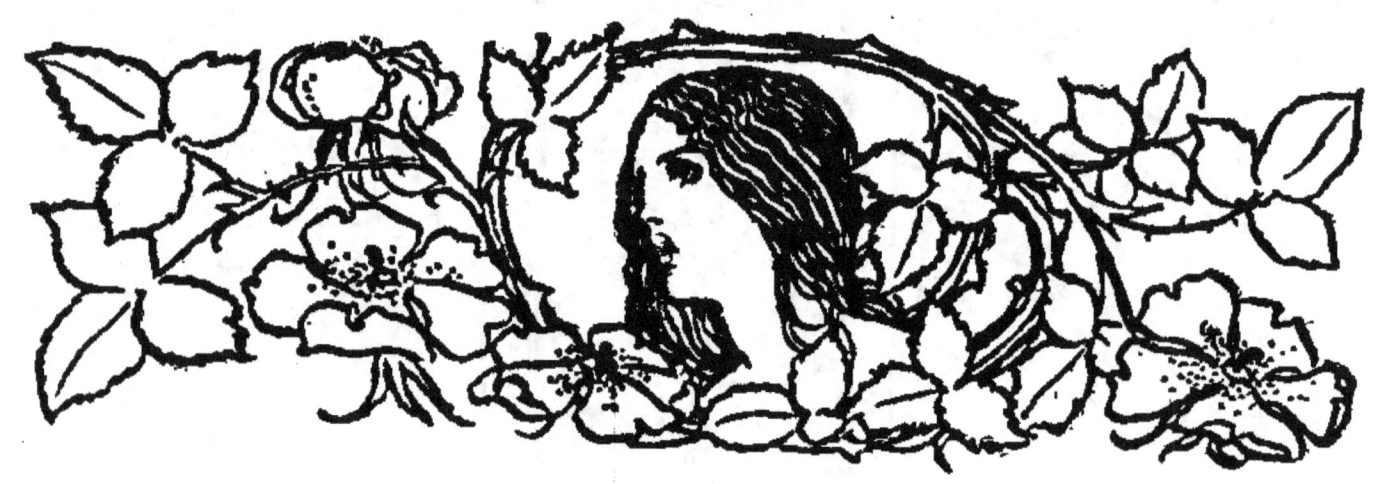

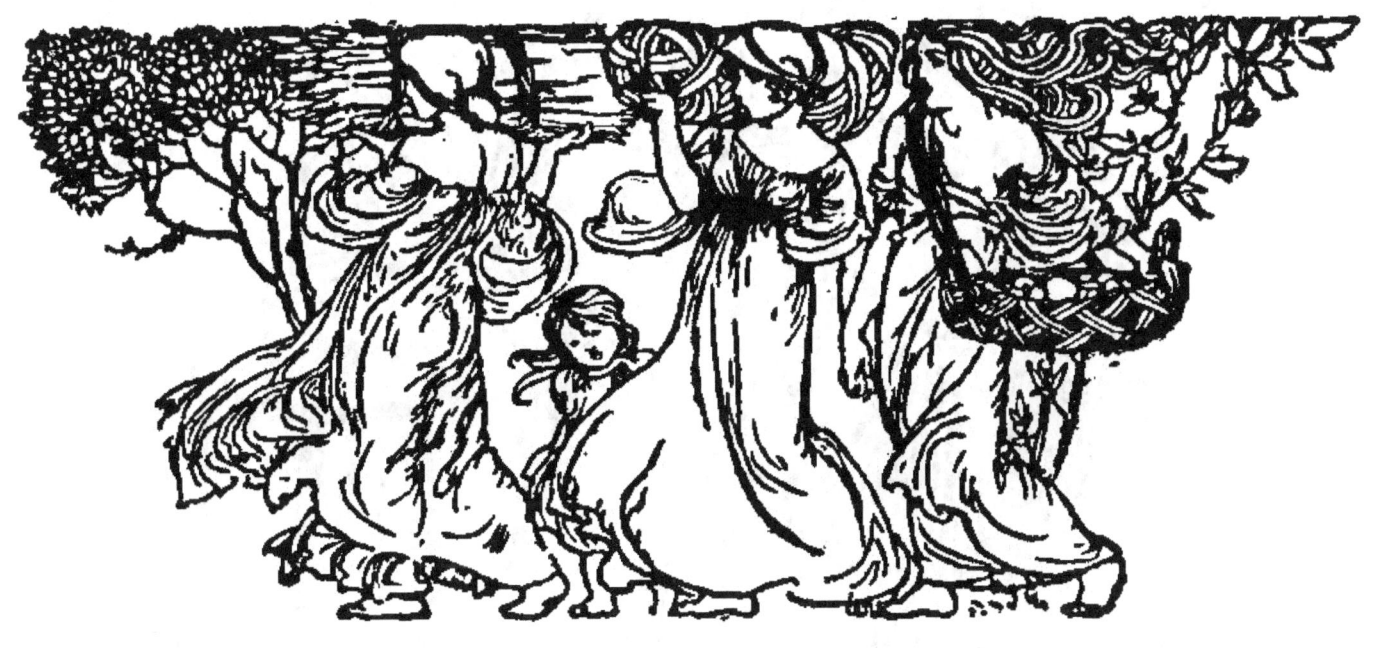

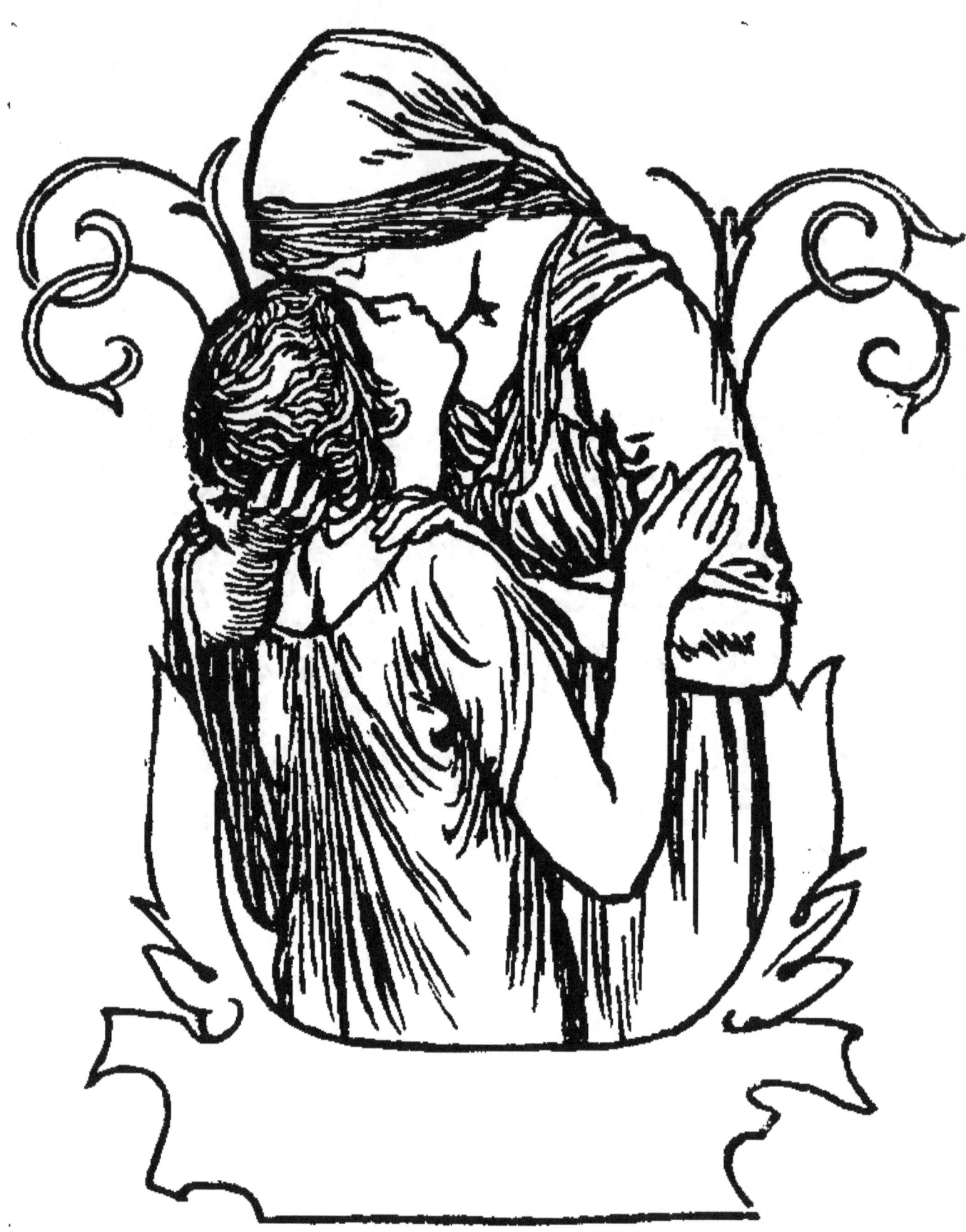

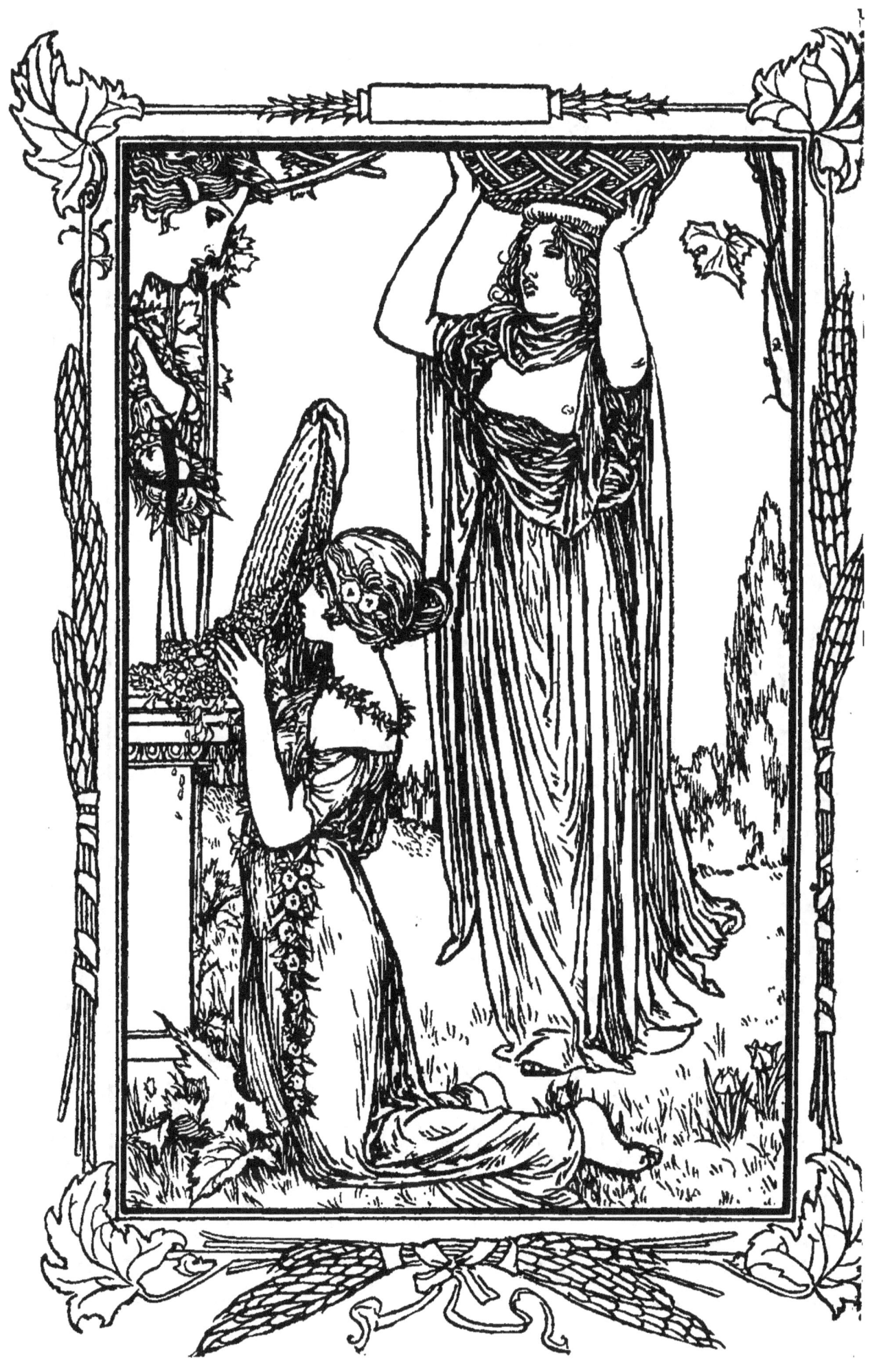

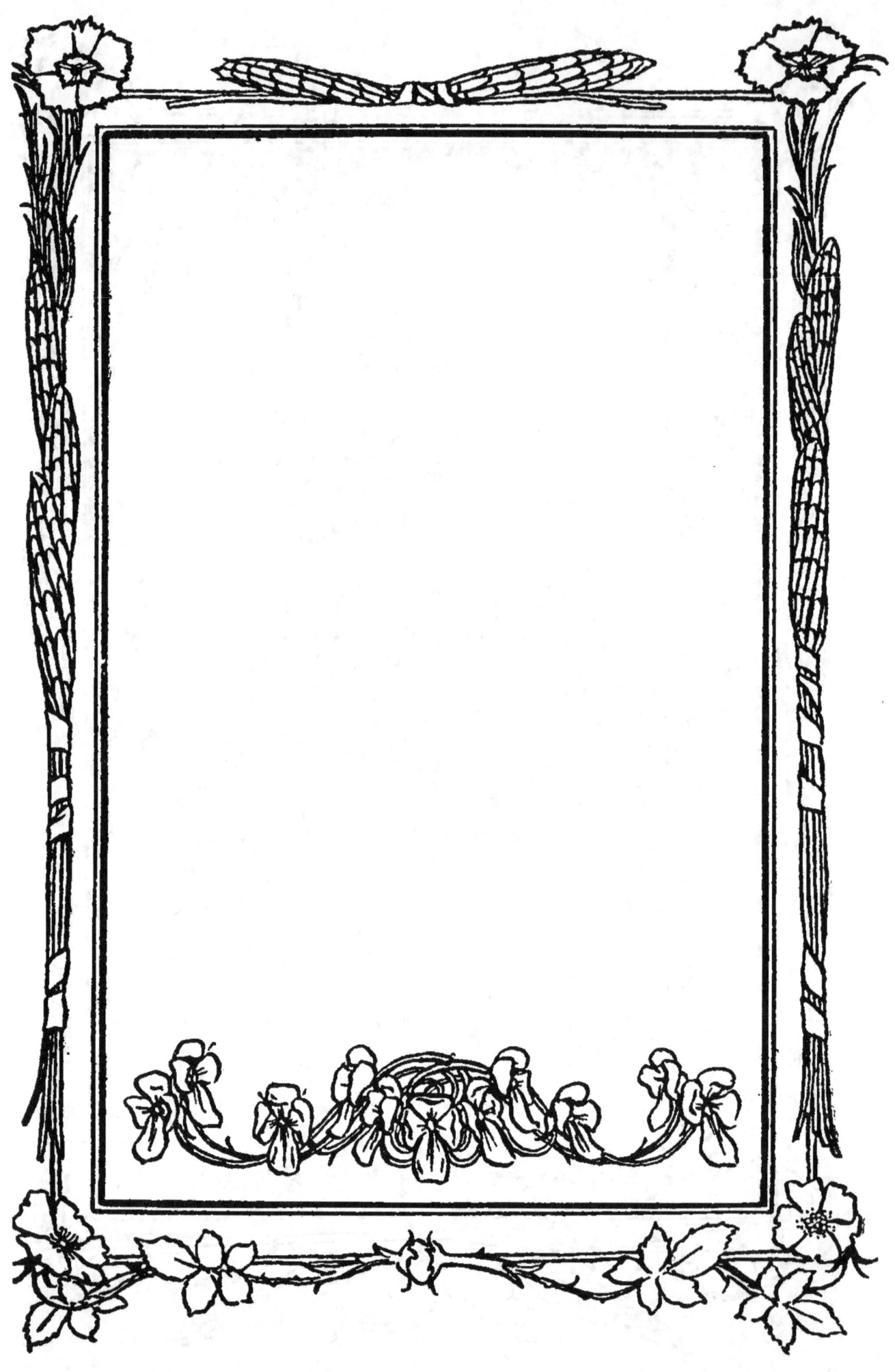

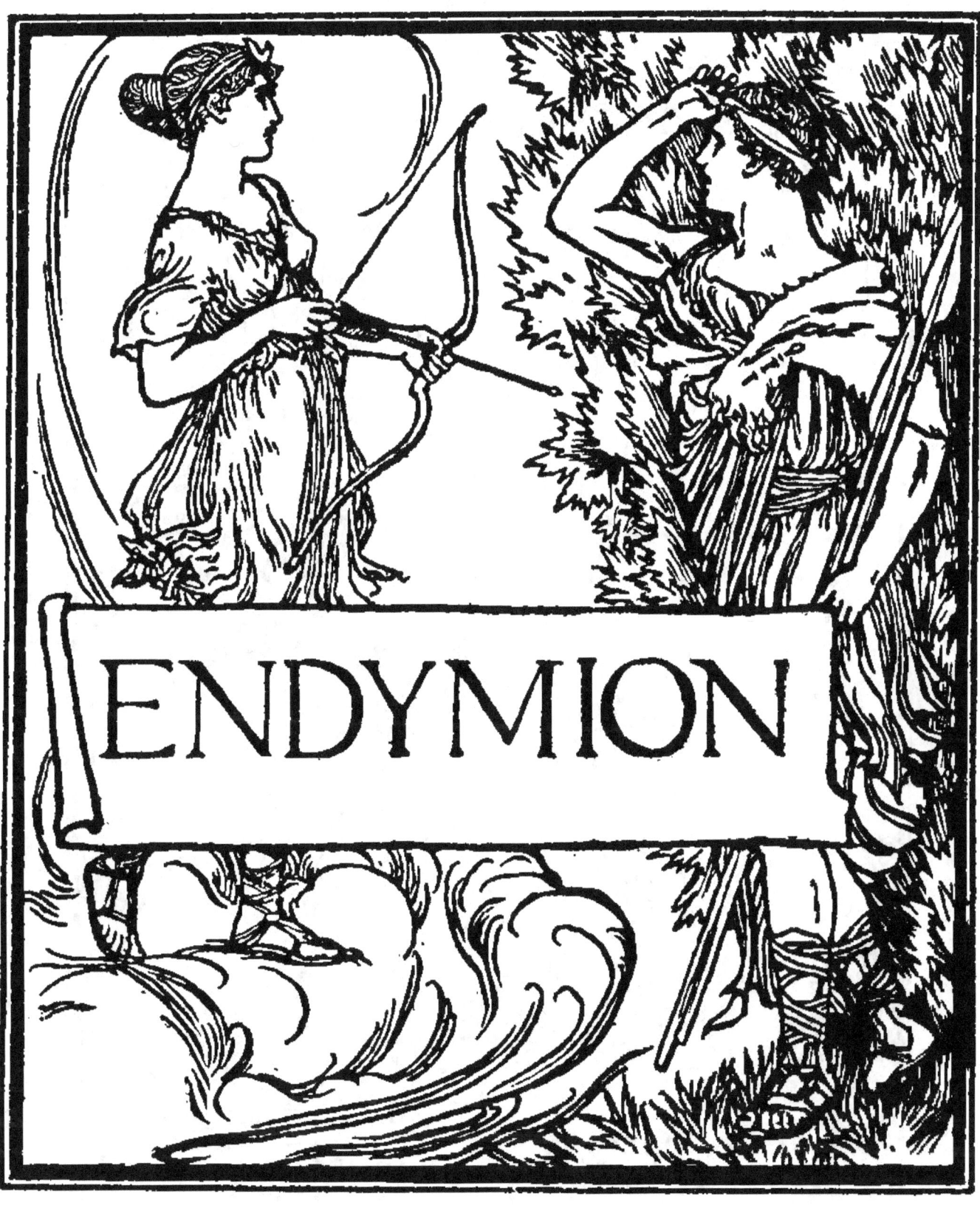

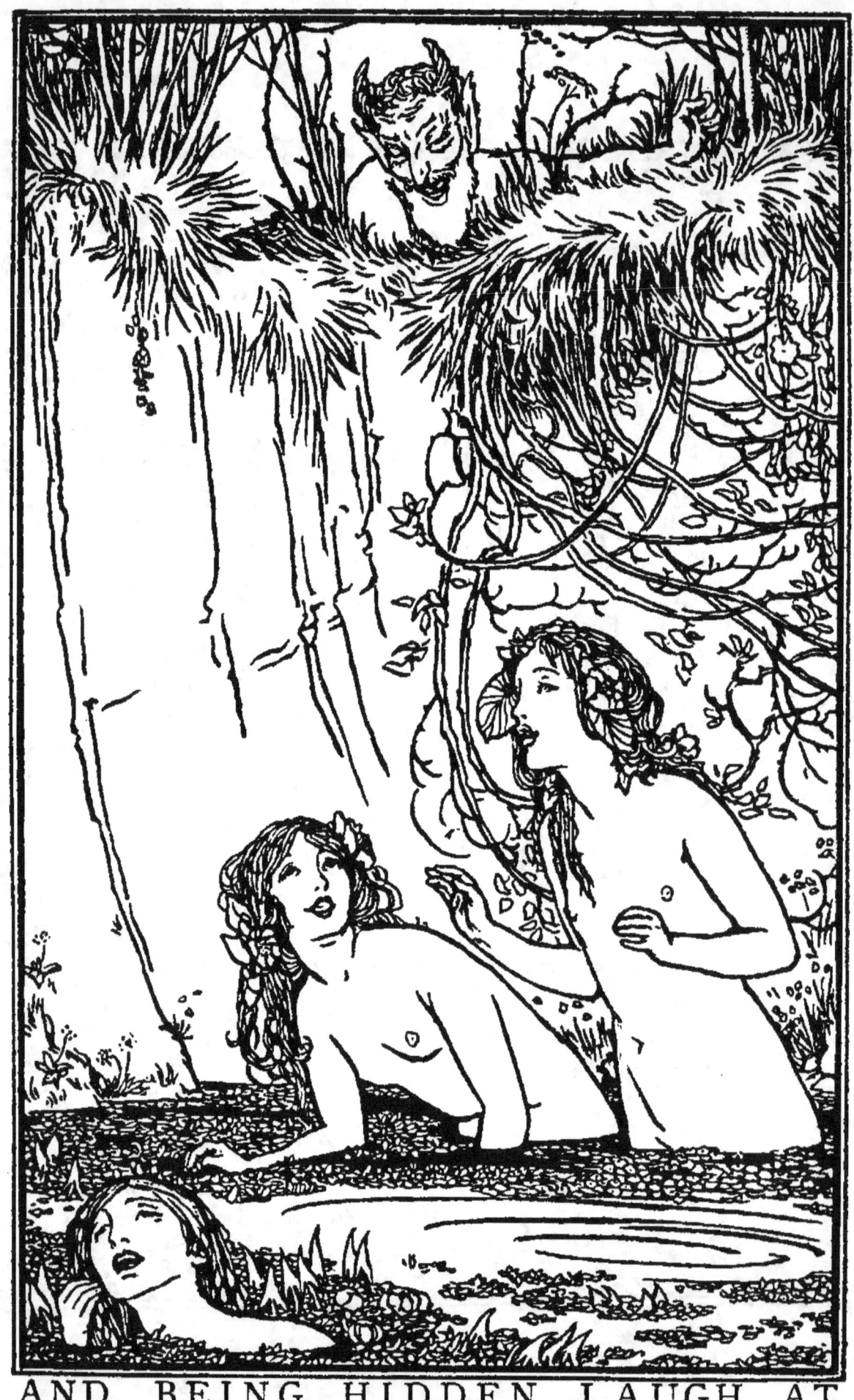

AND, BEING HIDDEN, LAUGH AT THEIR OUT-PEEPING

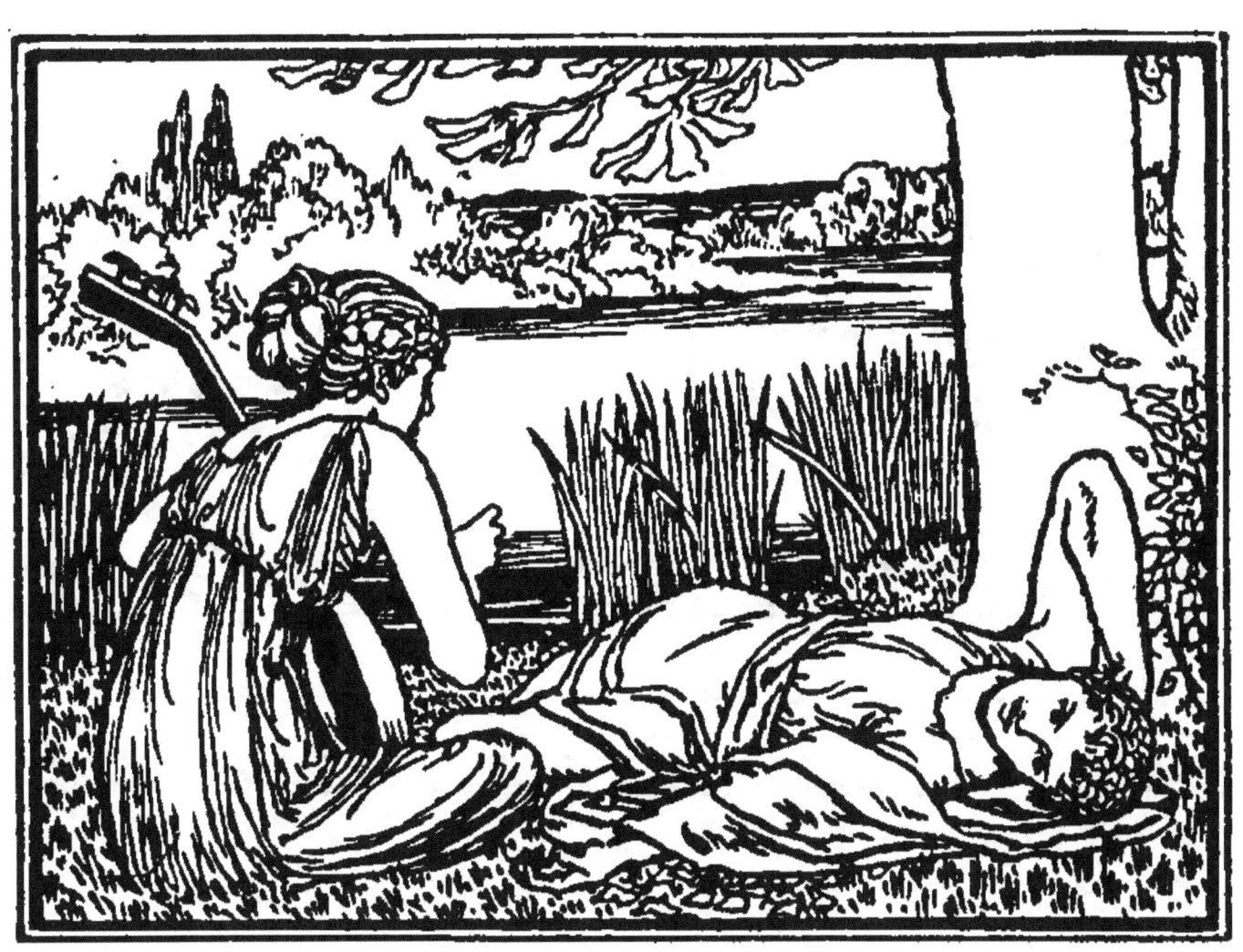

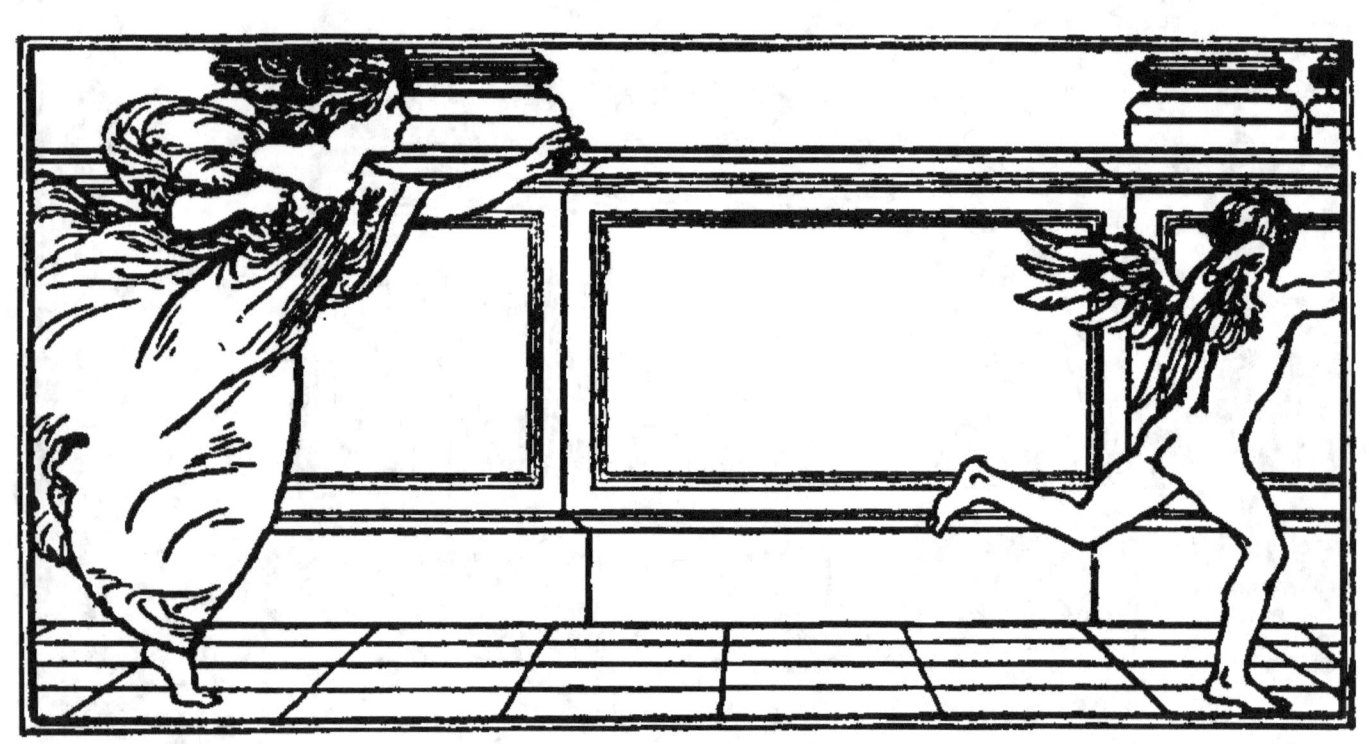

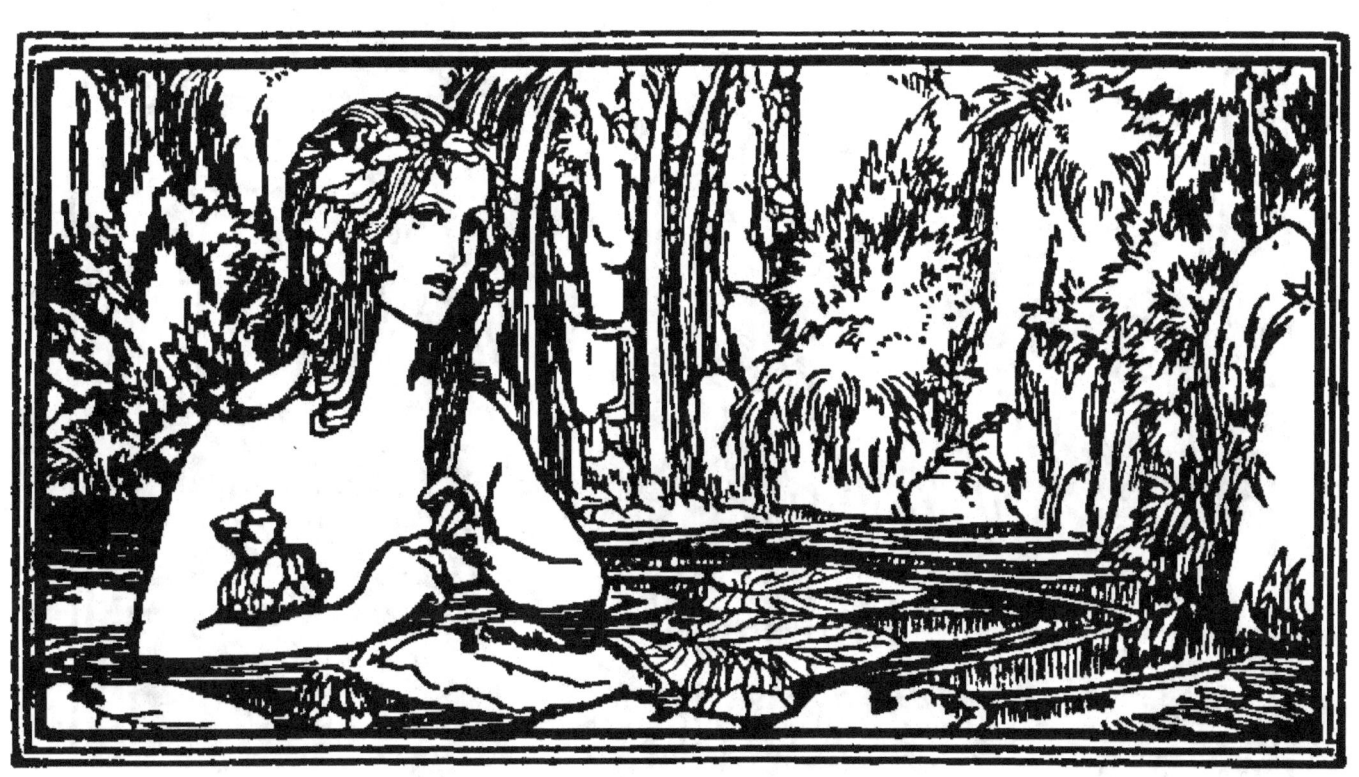

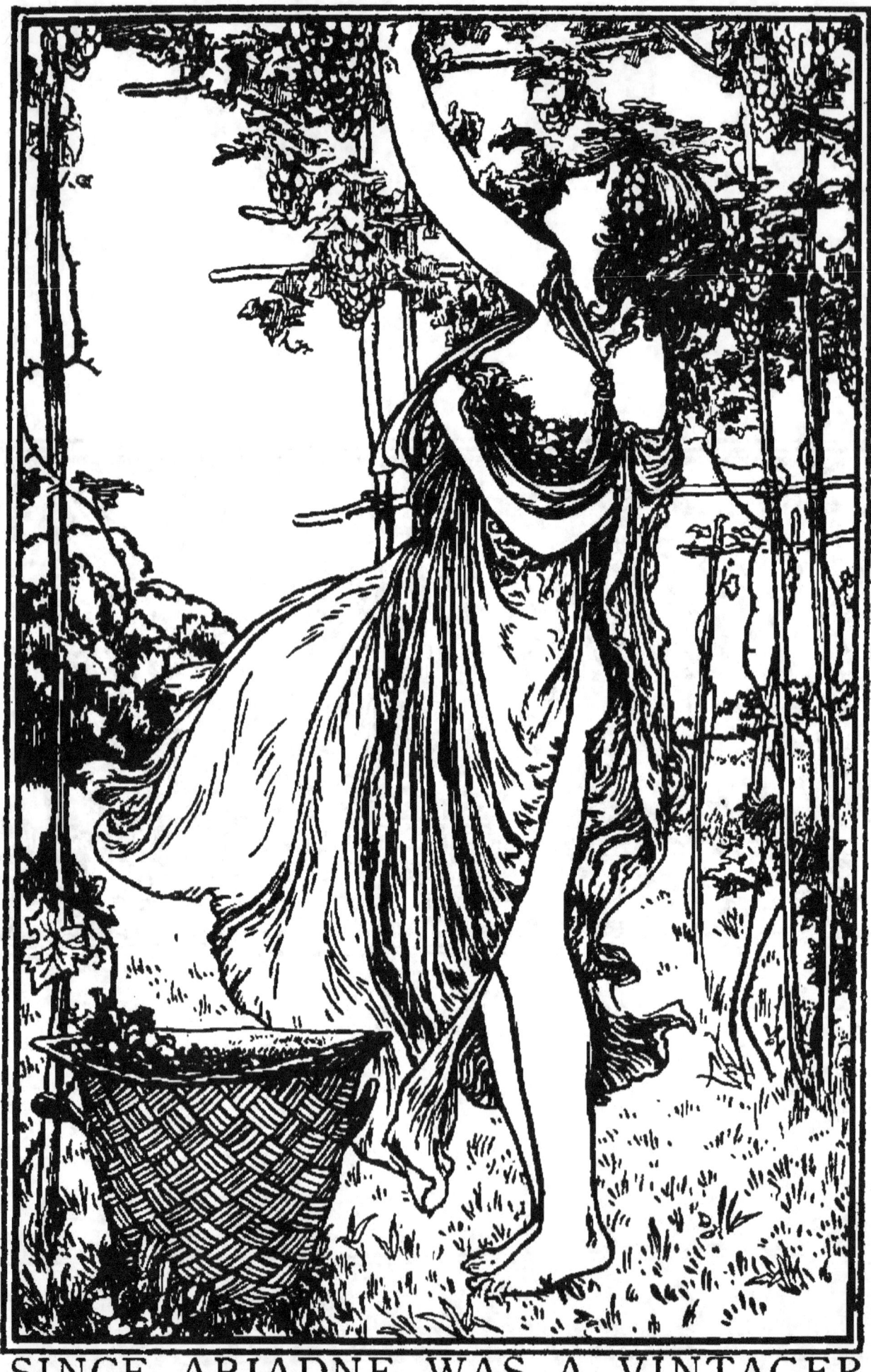
SINCE ARIADNE WAS A VINTAGER

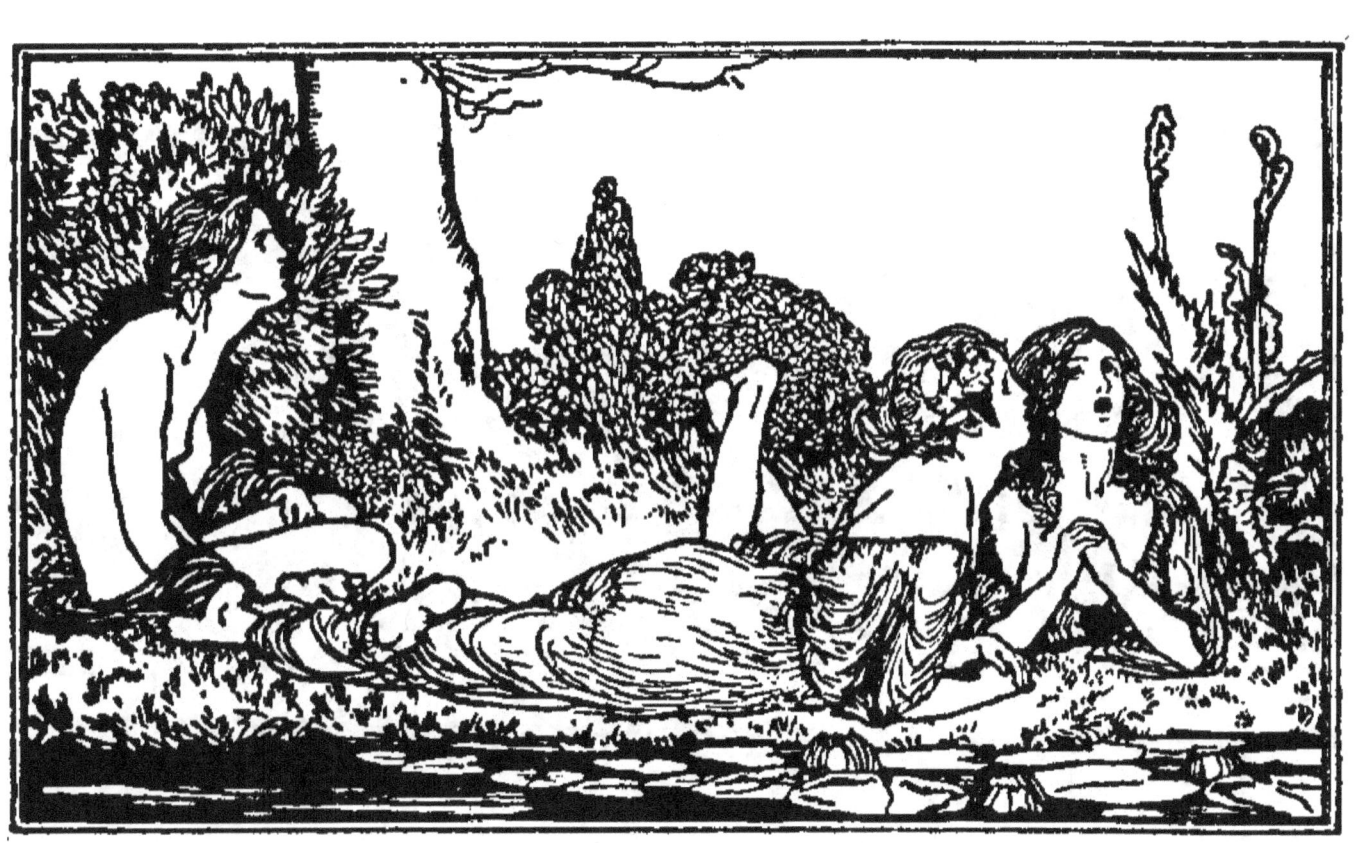

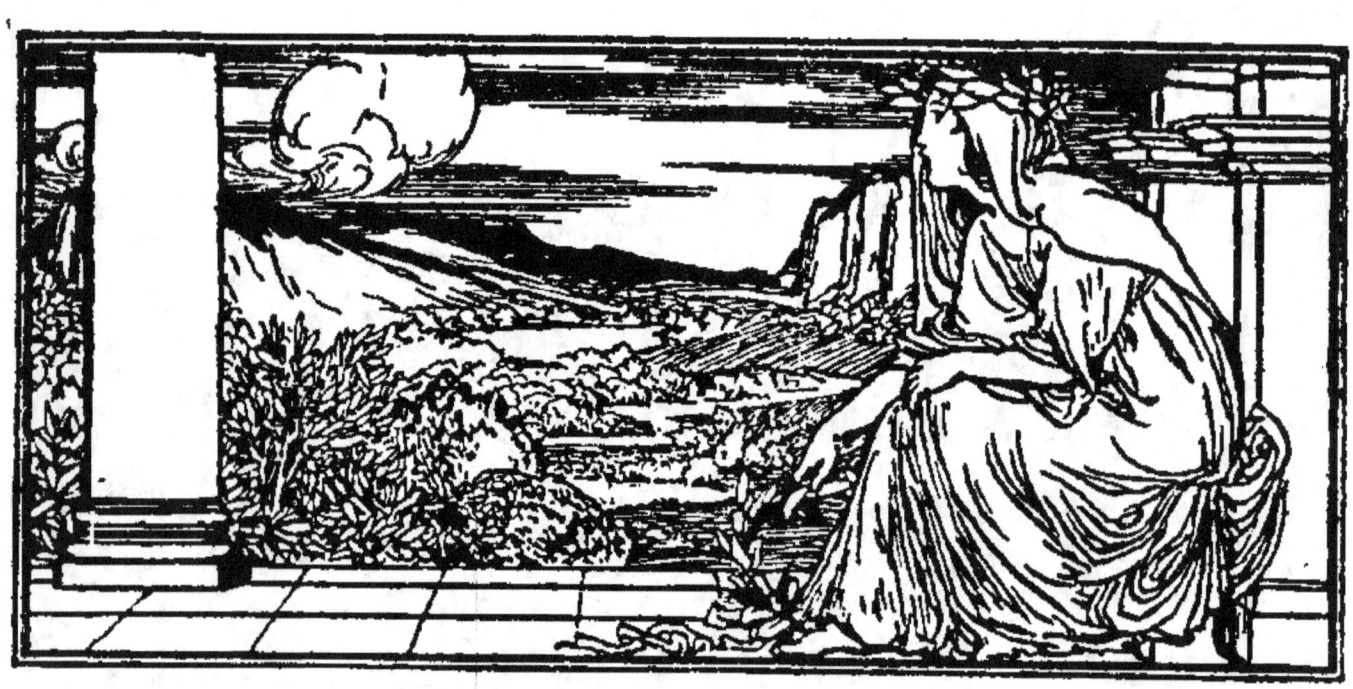

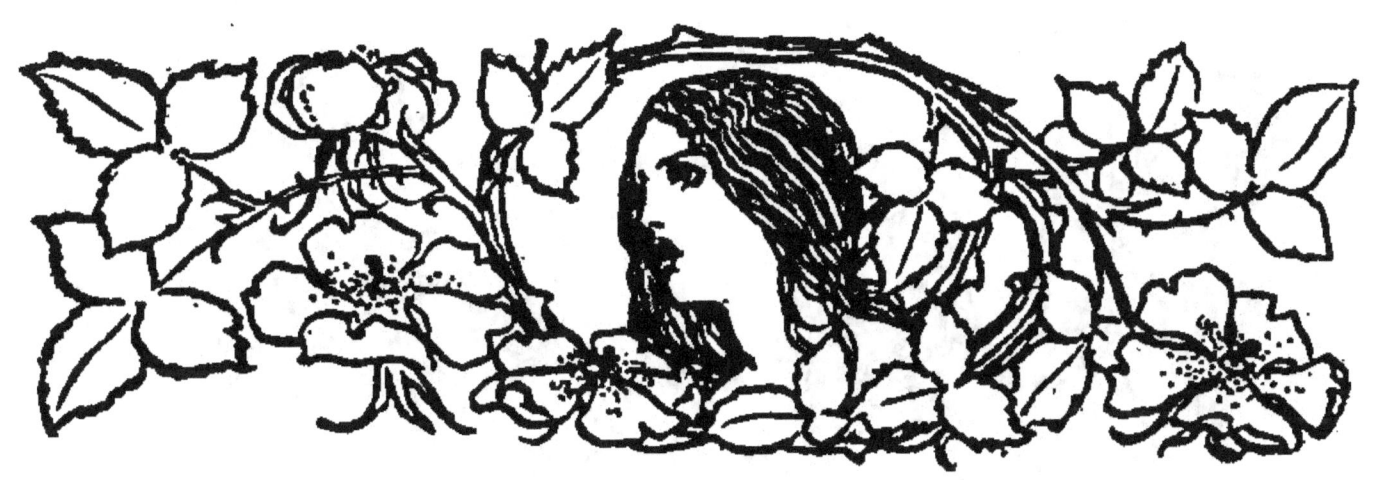

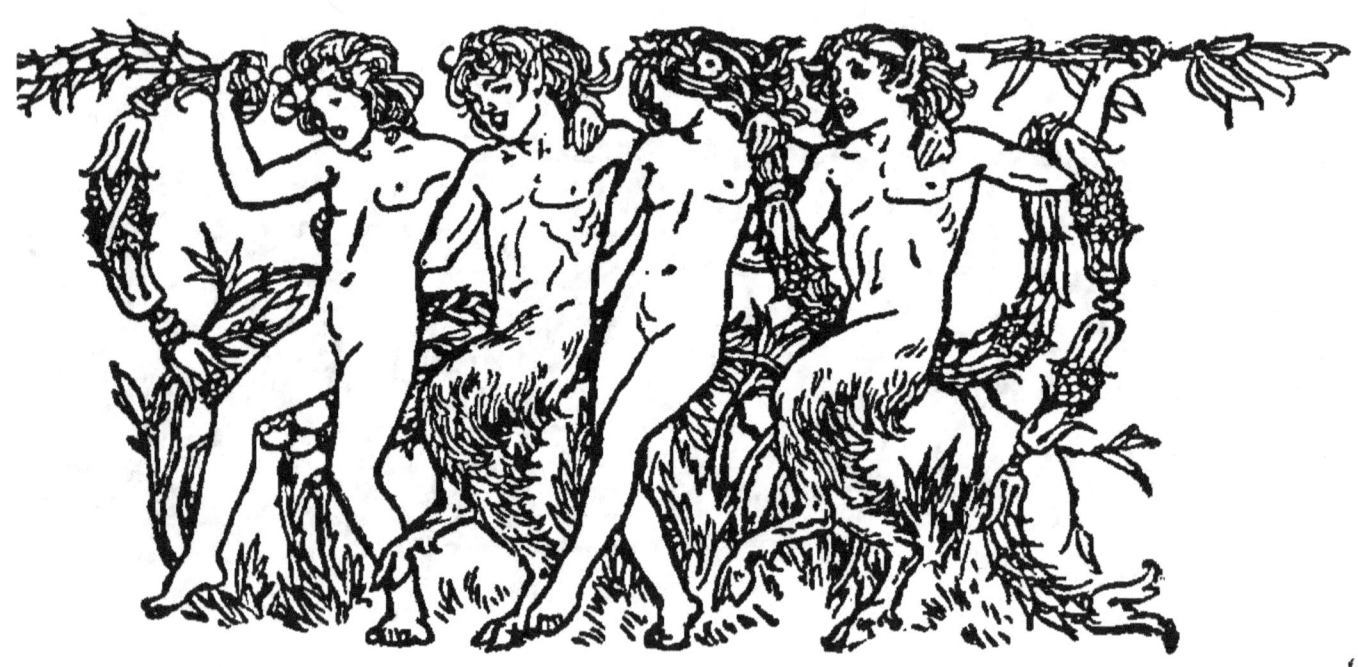

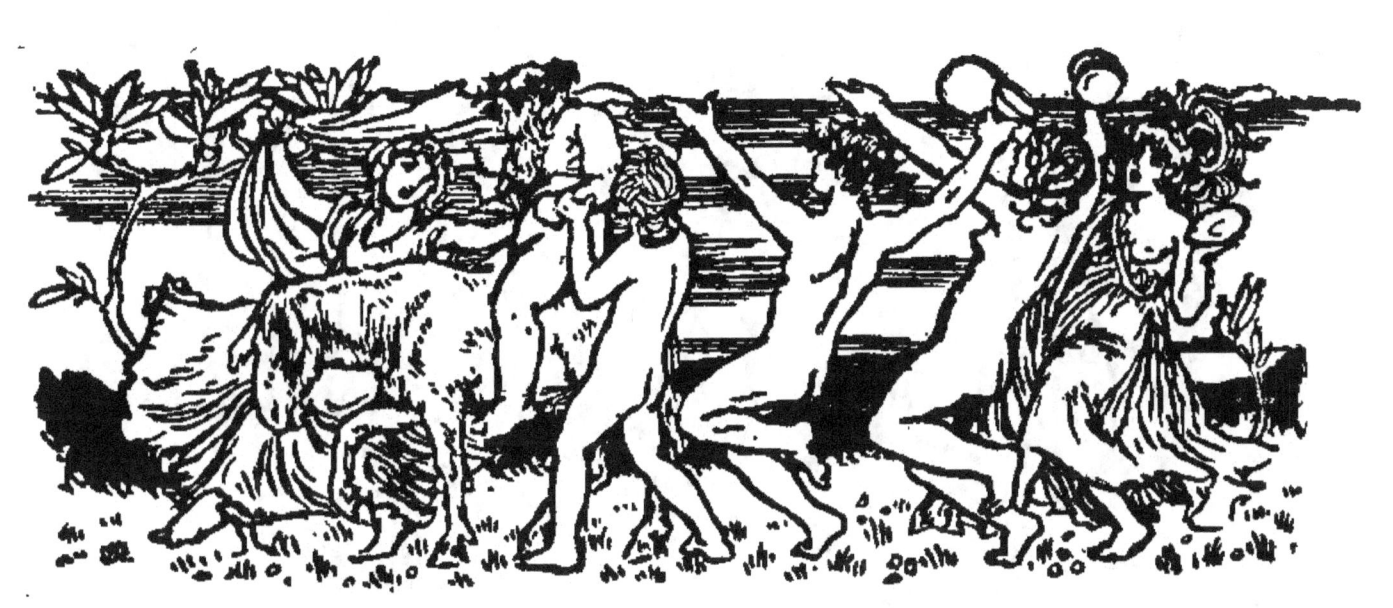

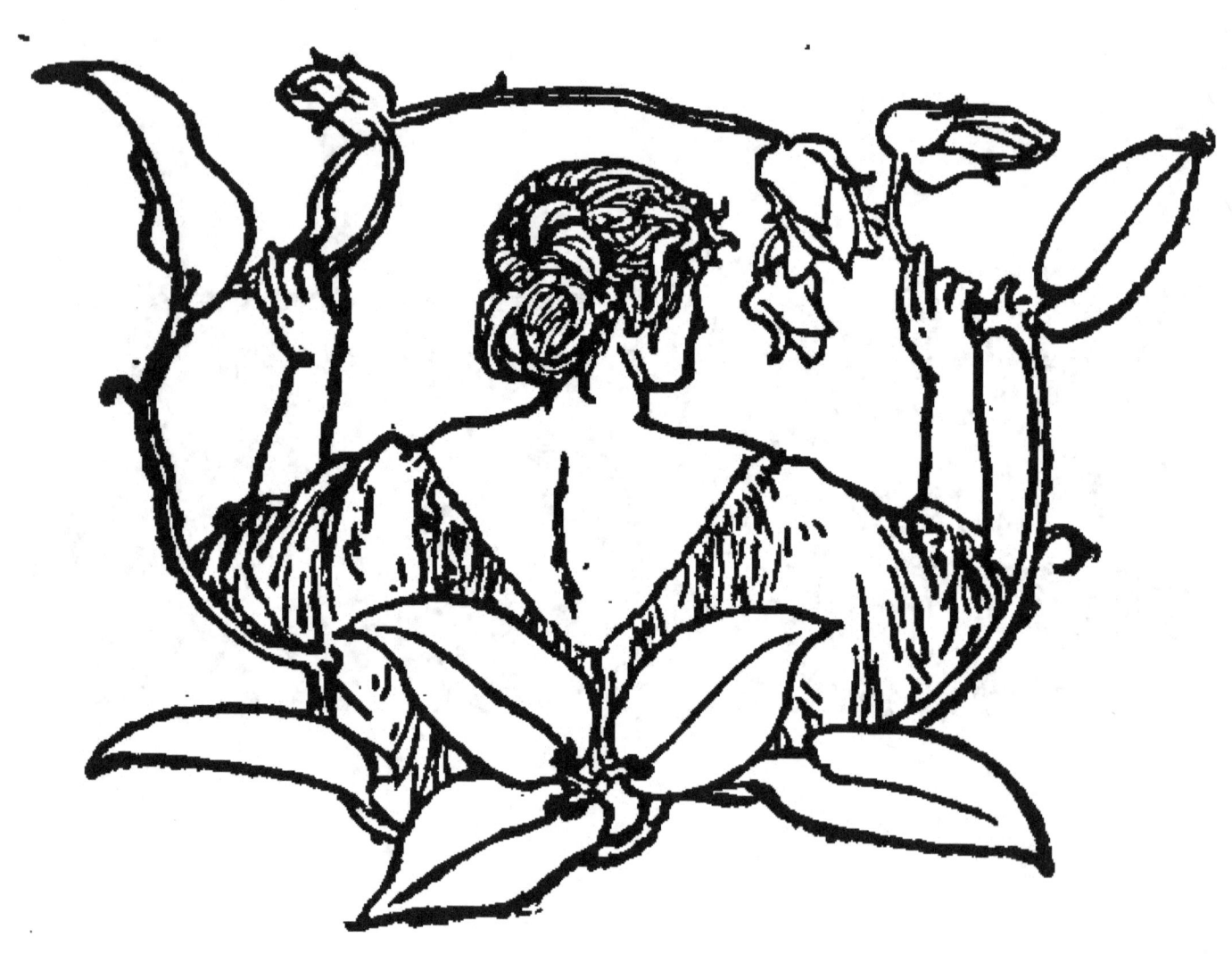

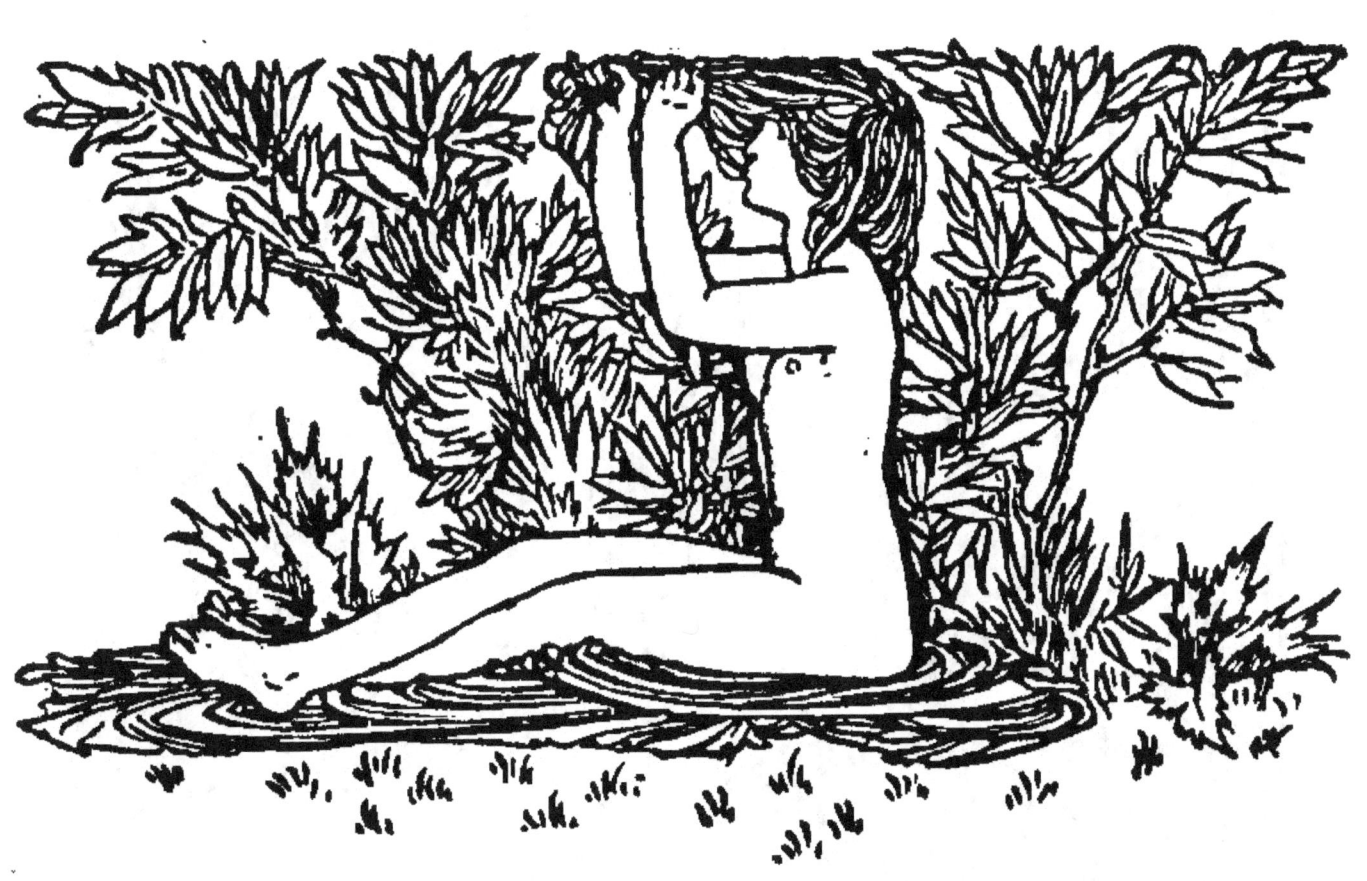

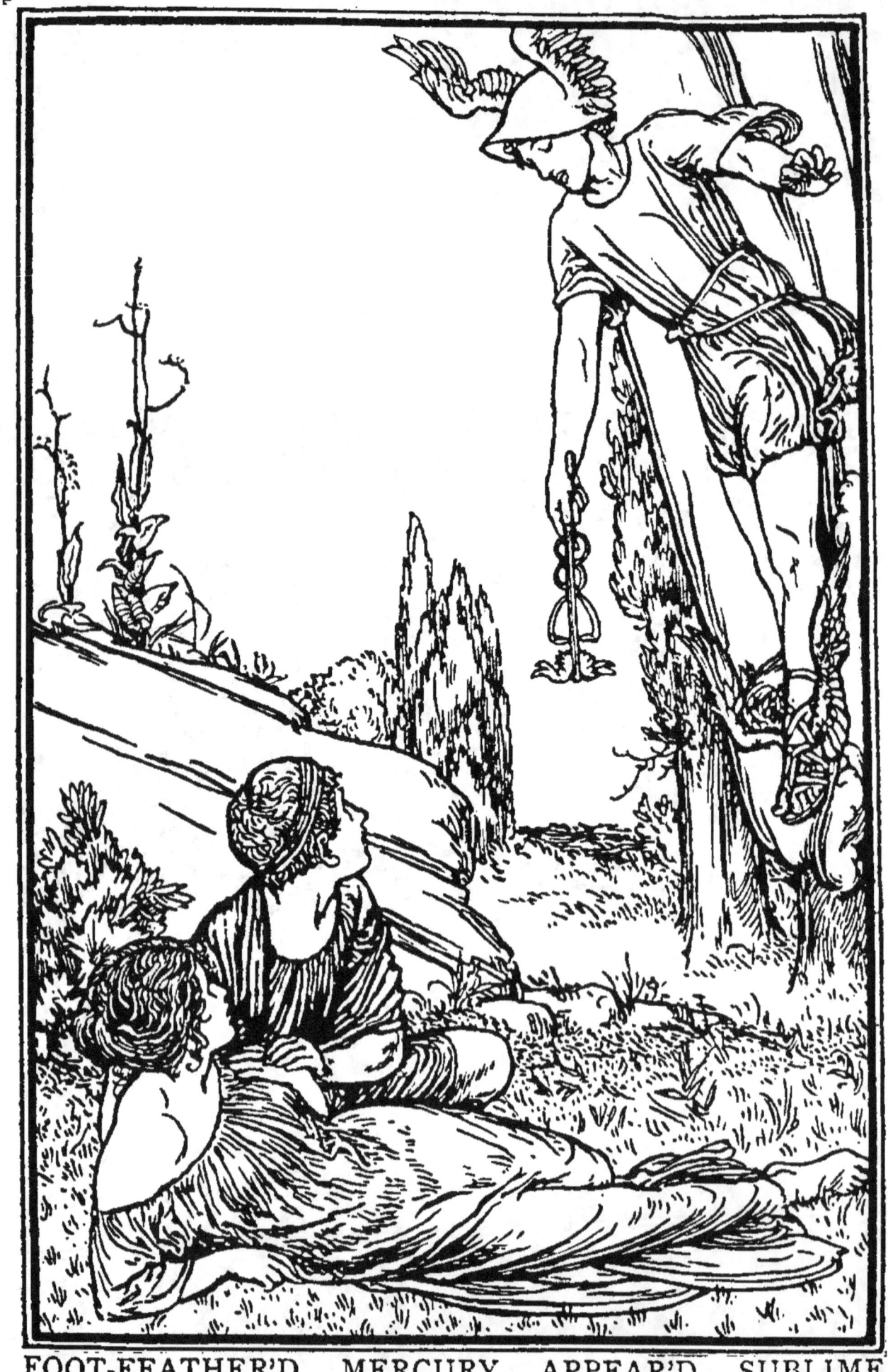

FOOT-FEATHER'D MERCURY APPEAR'D SUBLIME

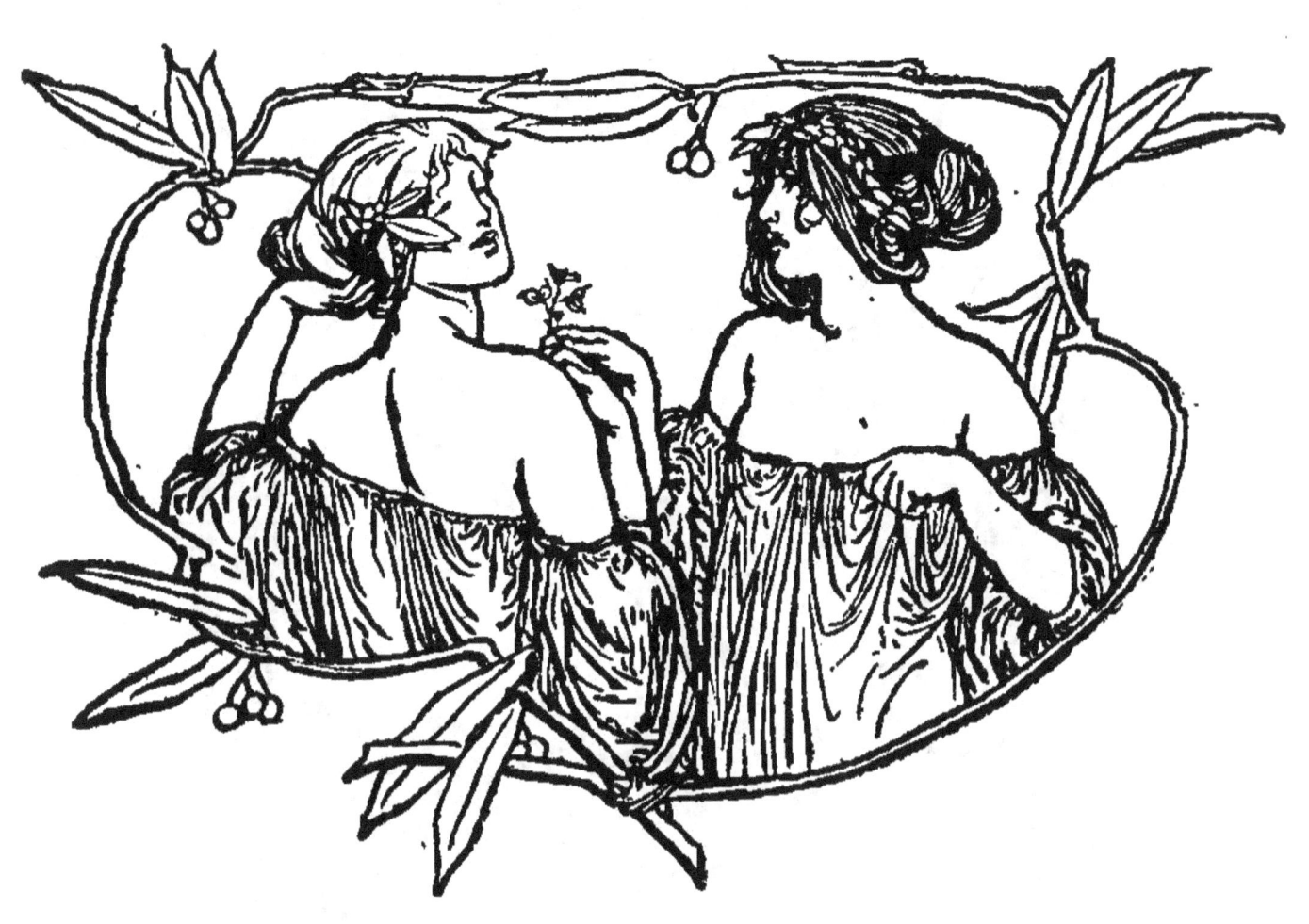

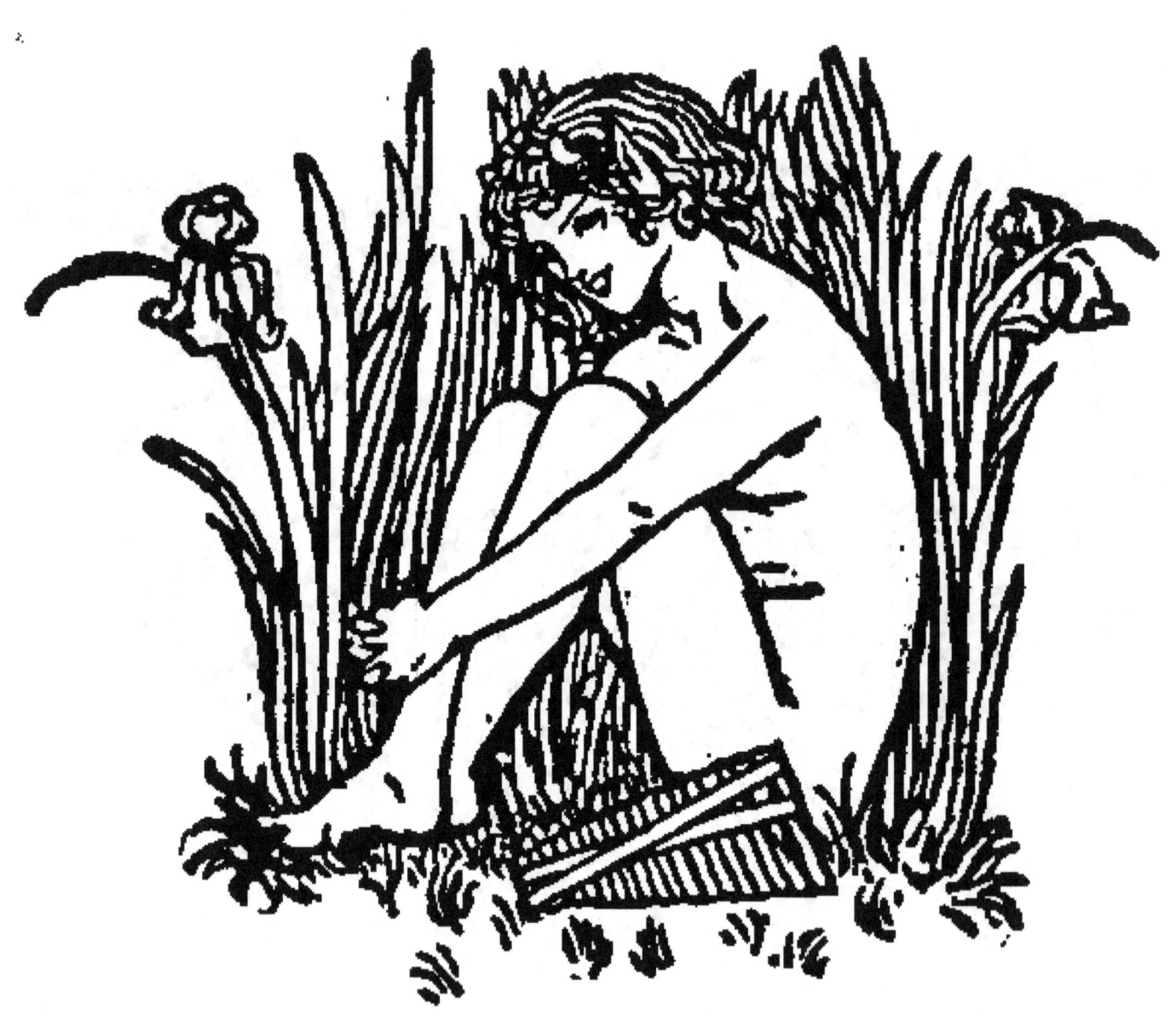

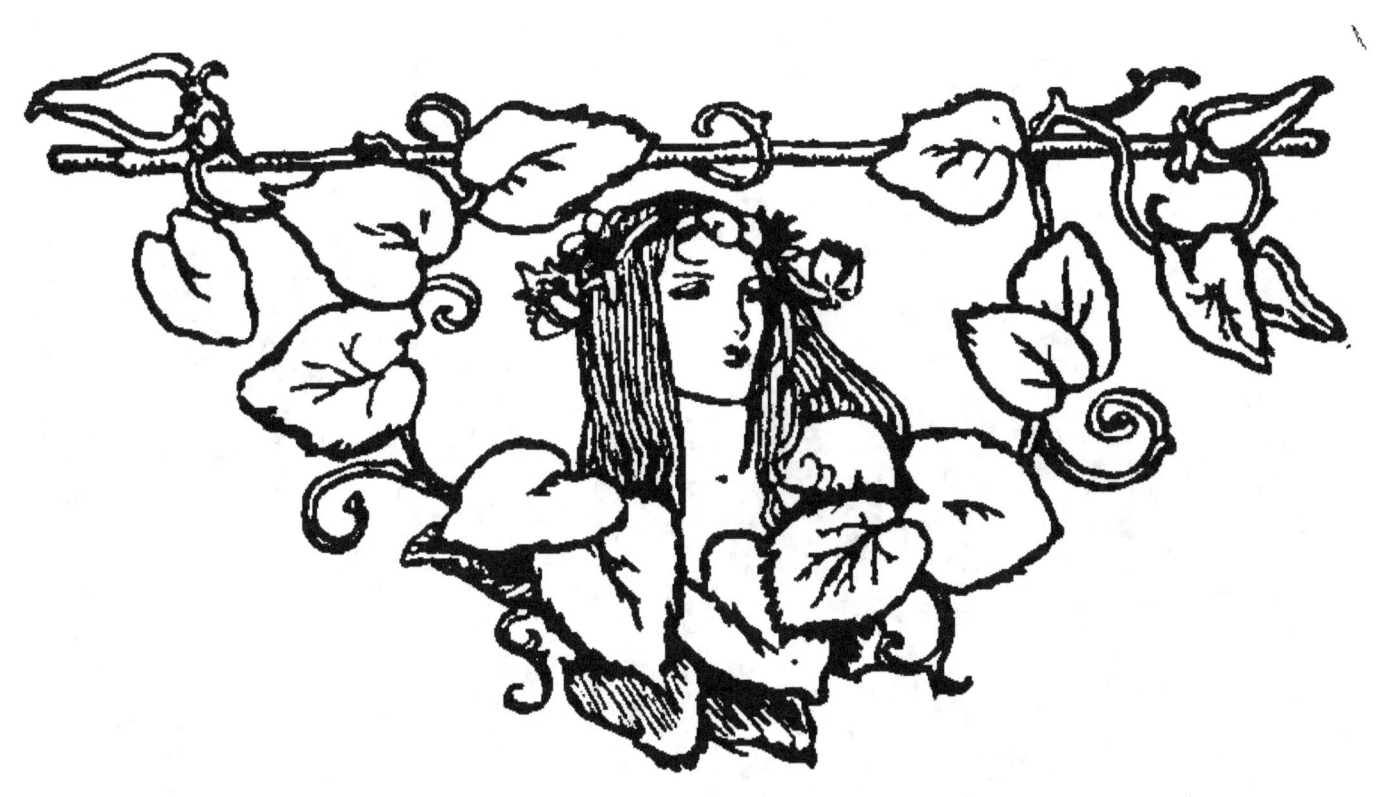

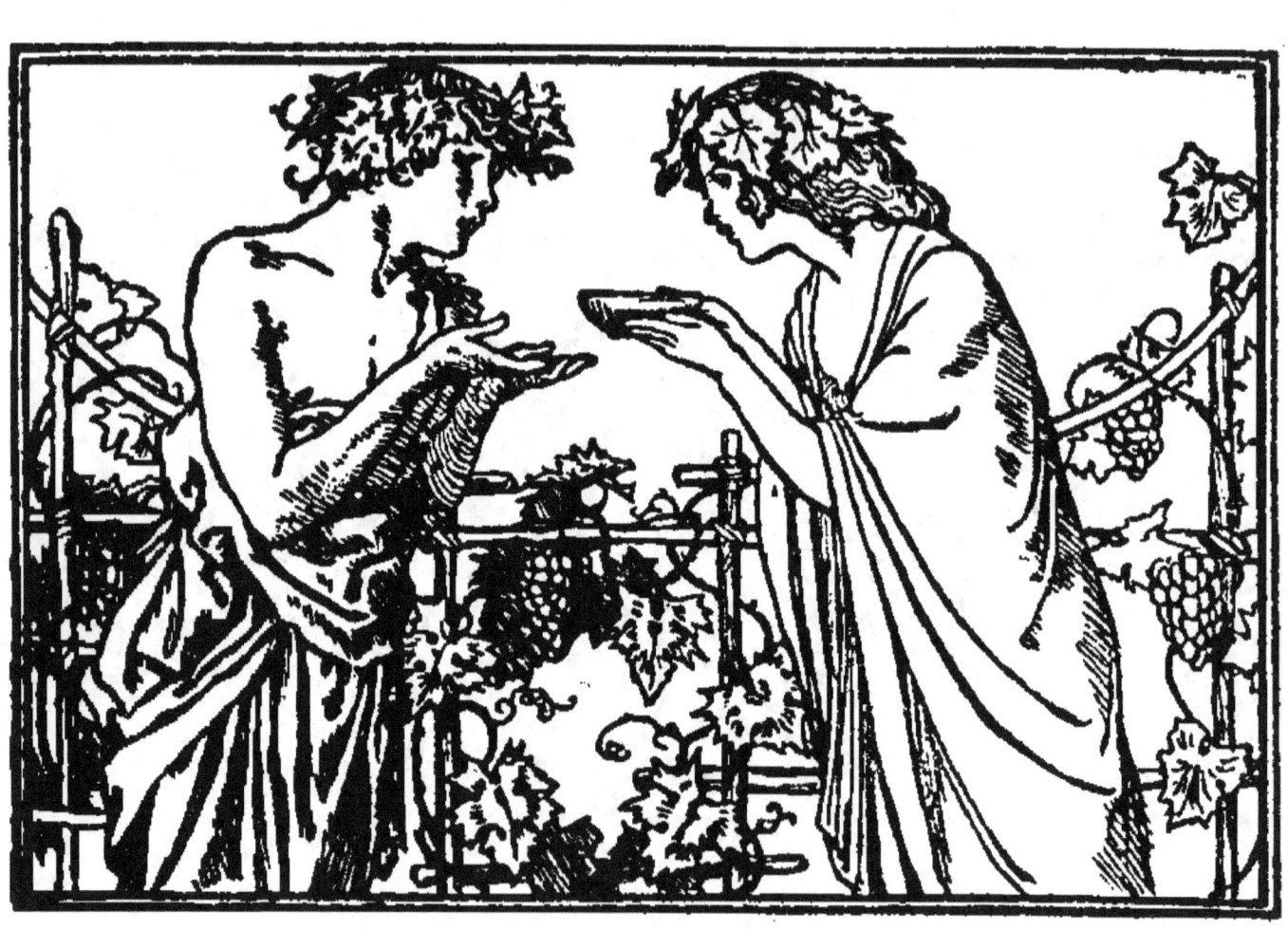

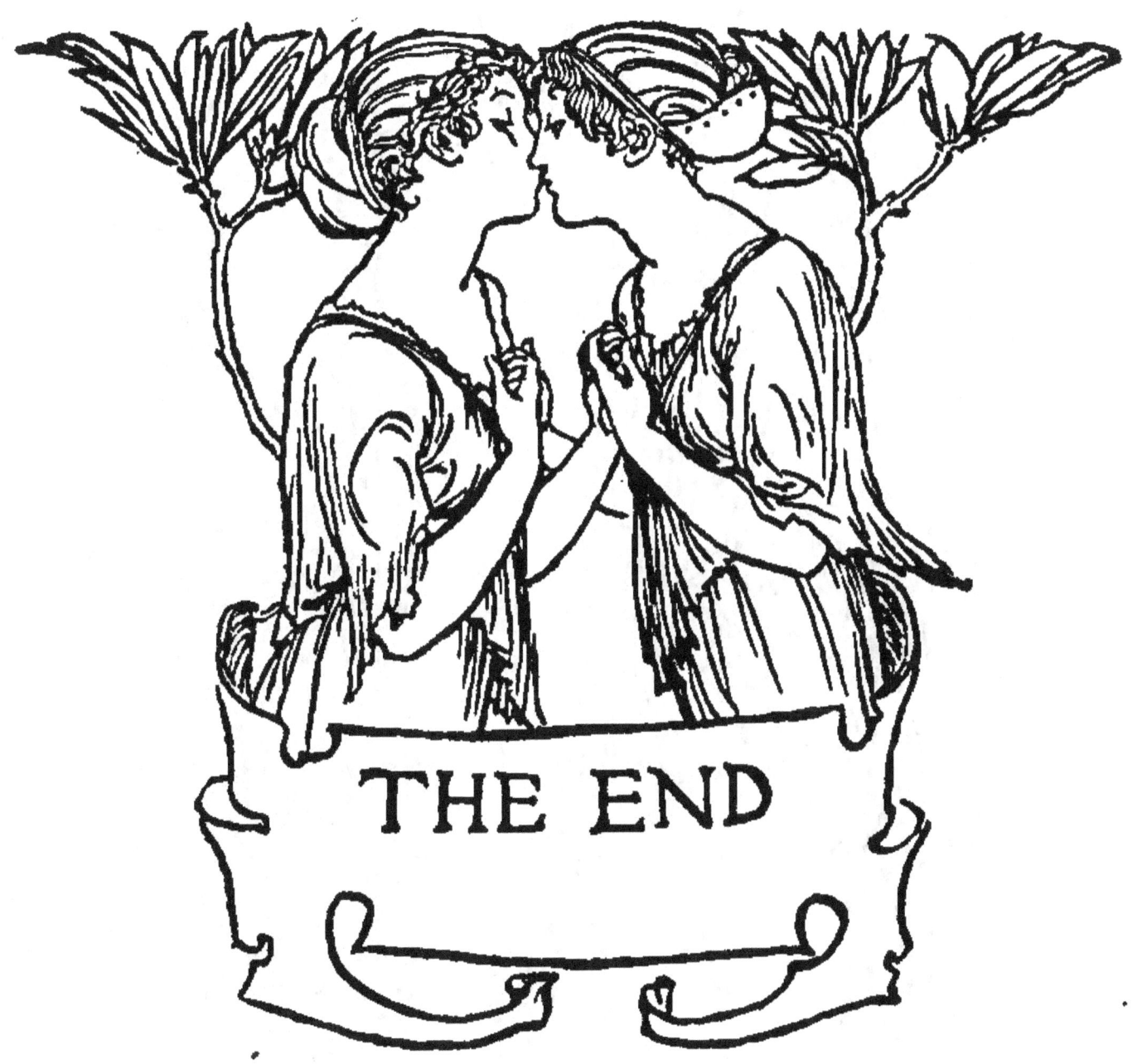

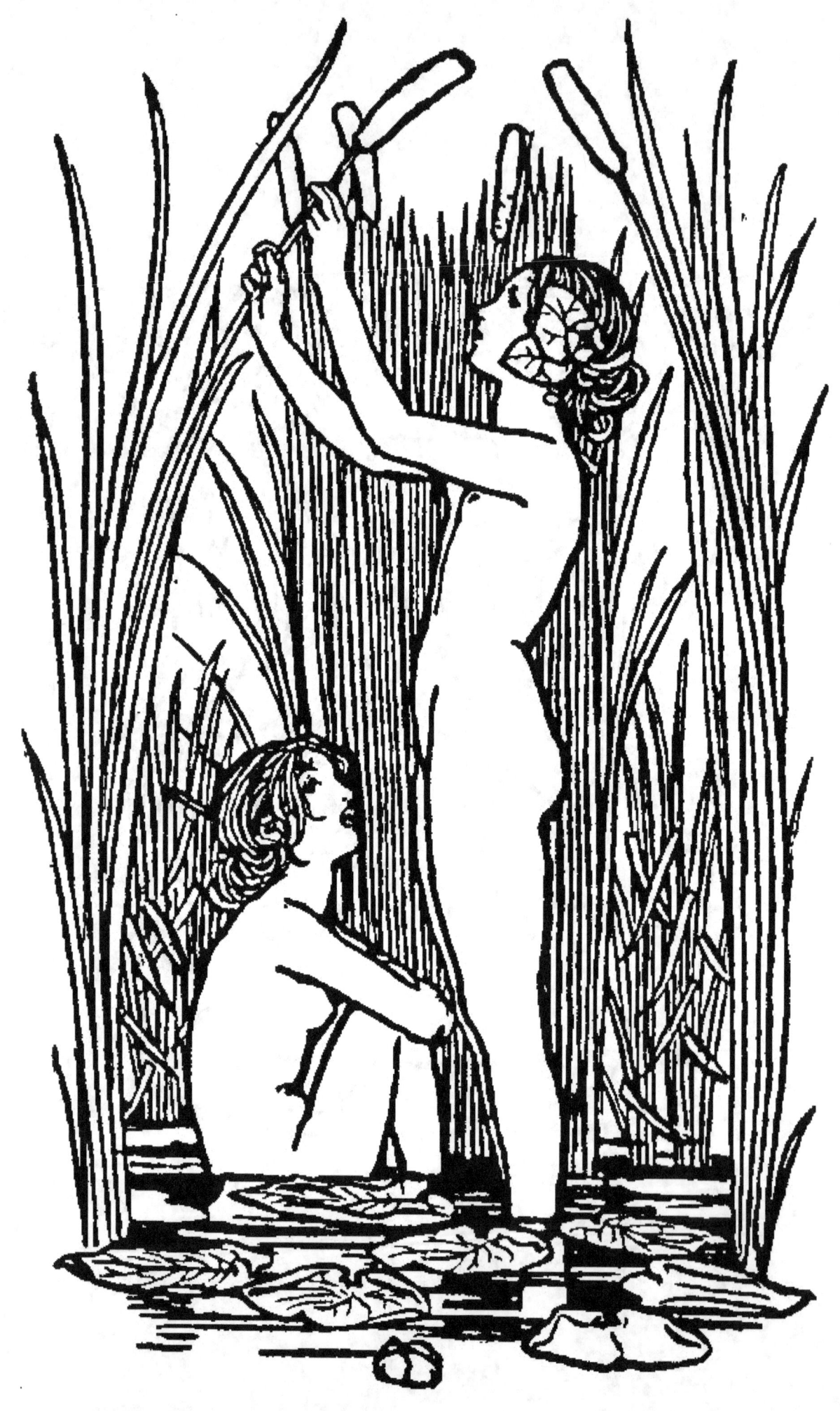

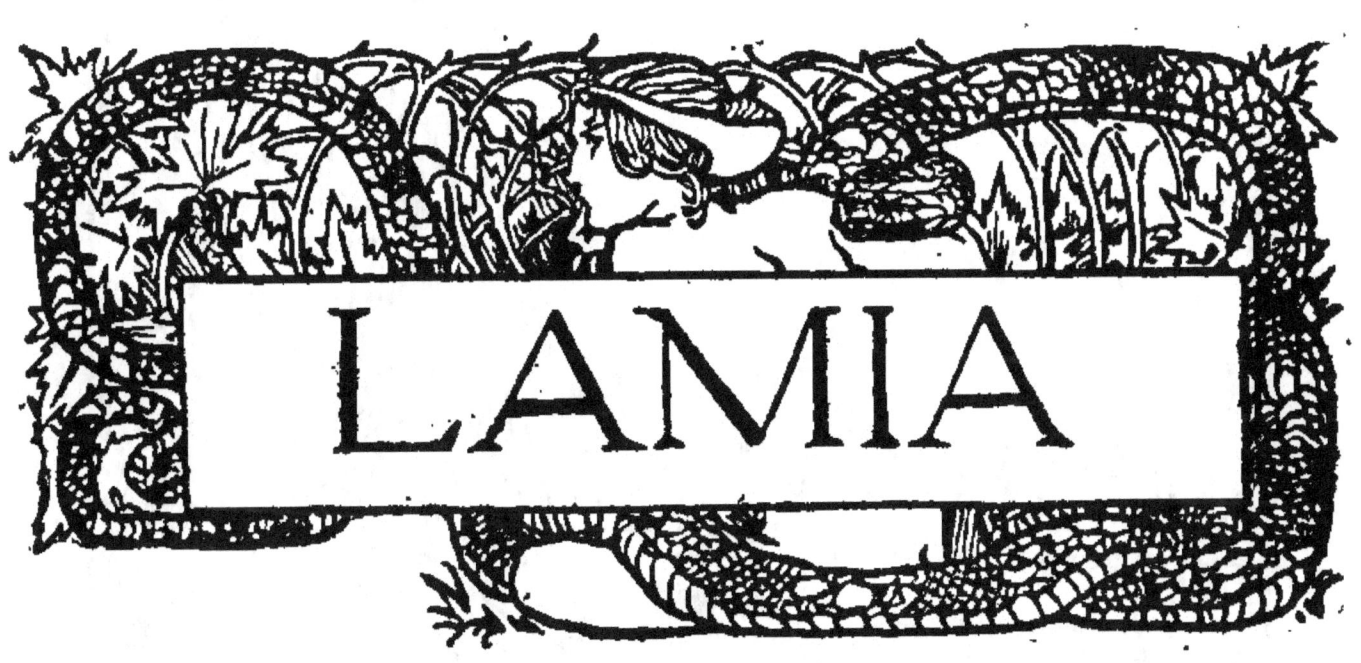

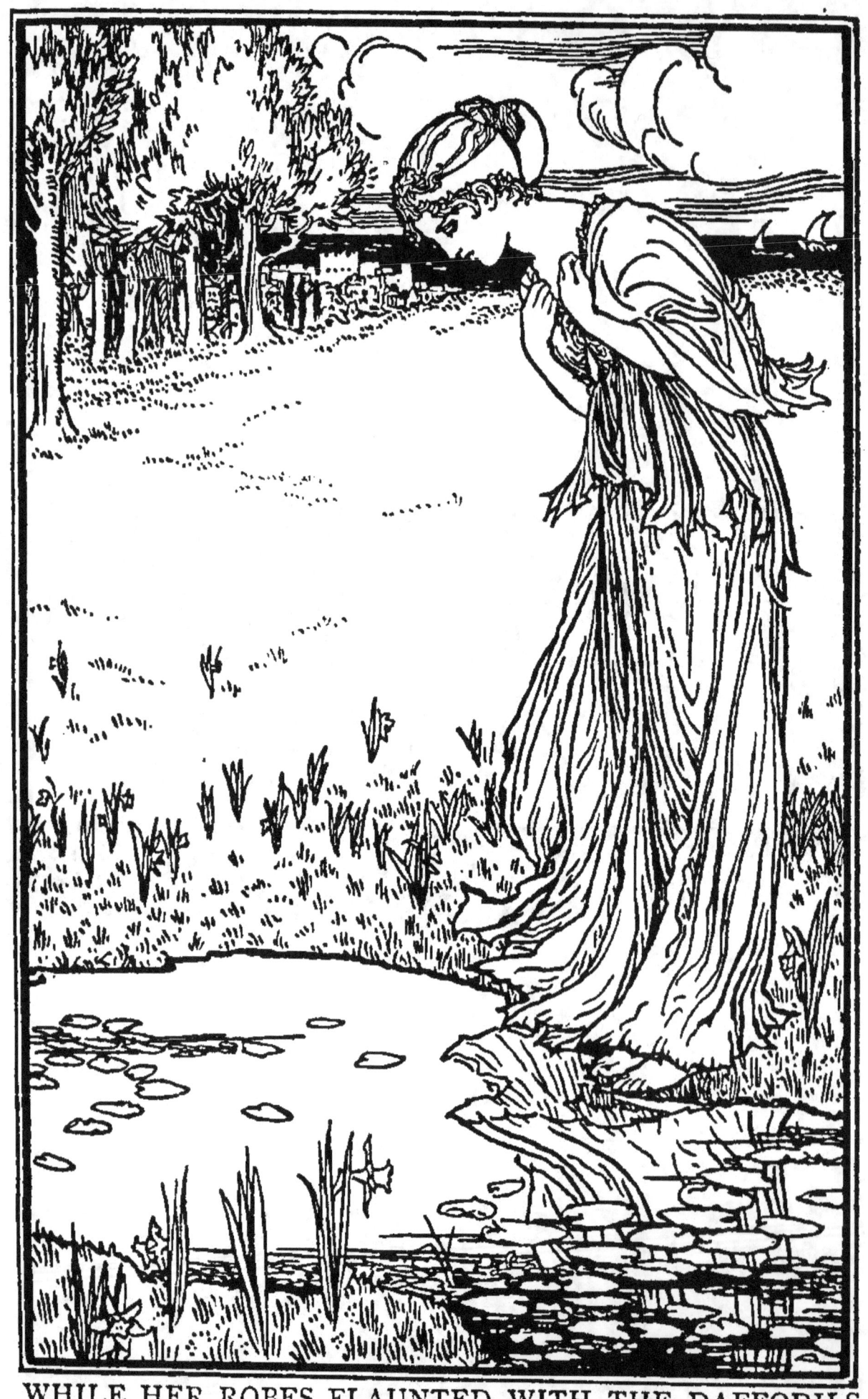

WHILE HER ROBES FLAUNTED WITH THE DAFFODILS

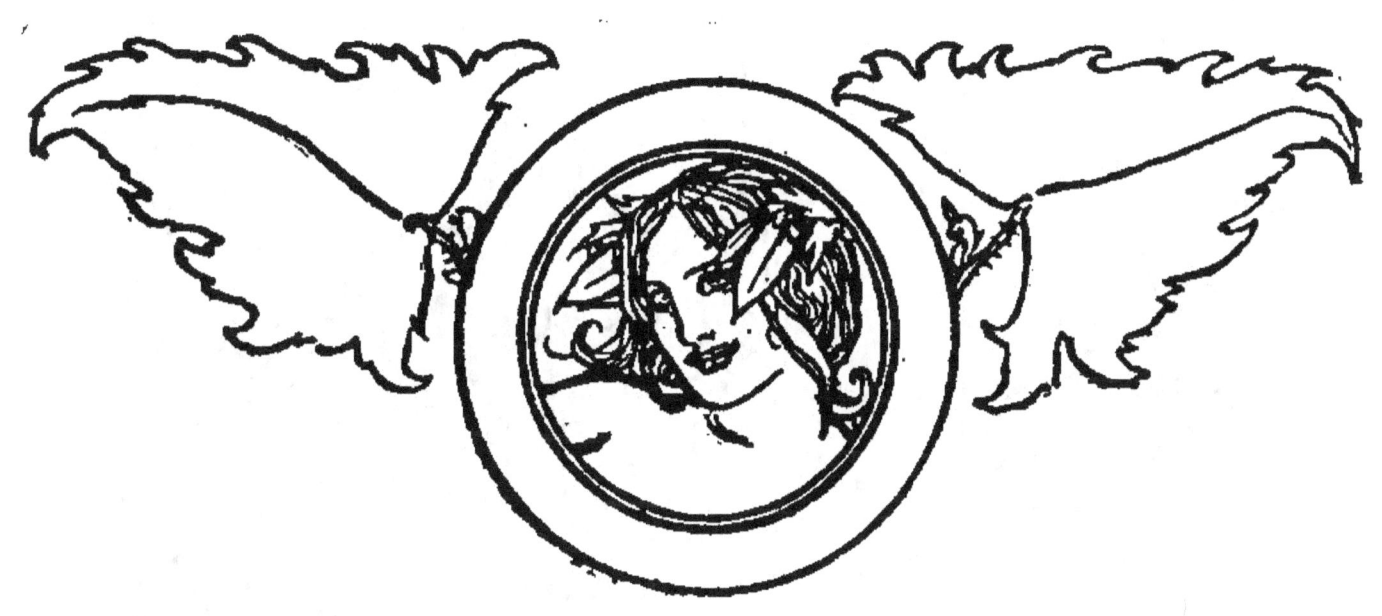

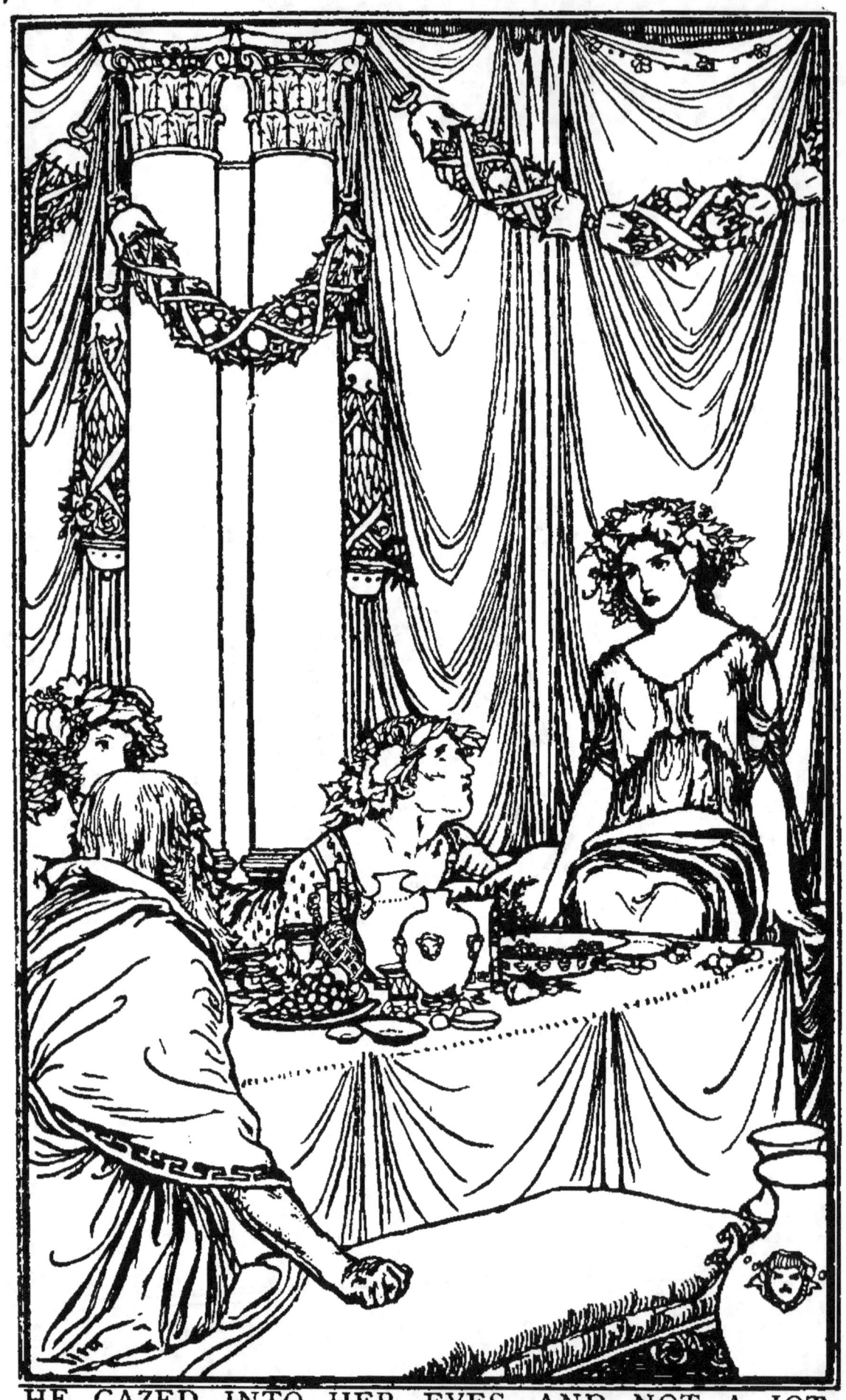

HE GAZED INTO HER EYES, AND NOT A JOT
OWN'D THEY THE LOVELORN PITEOUS APPEAL

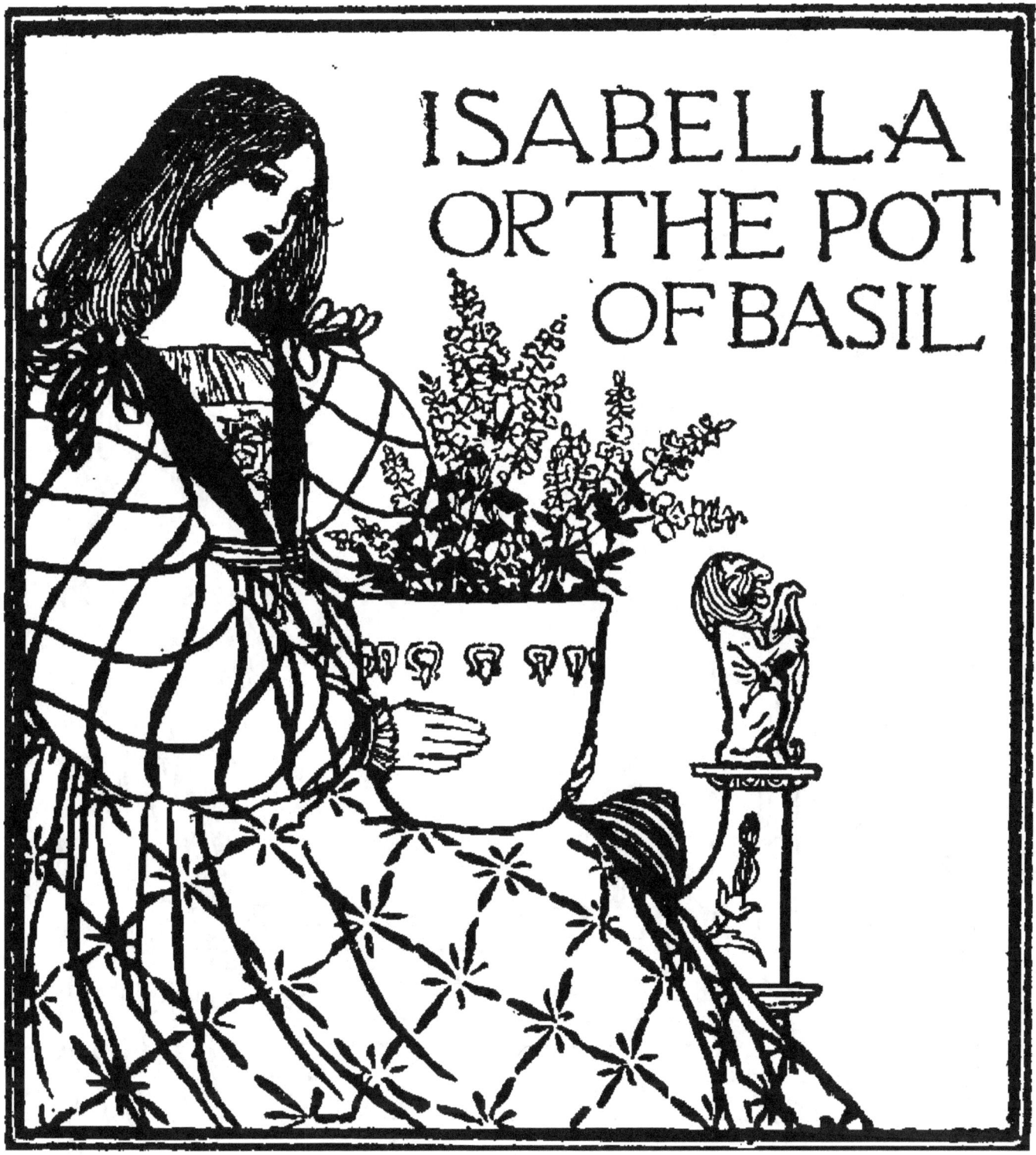

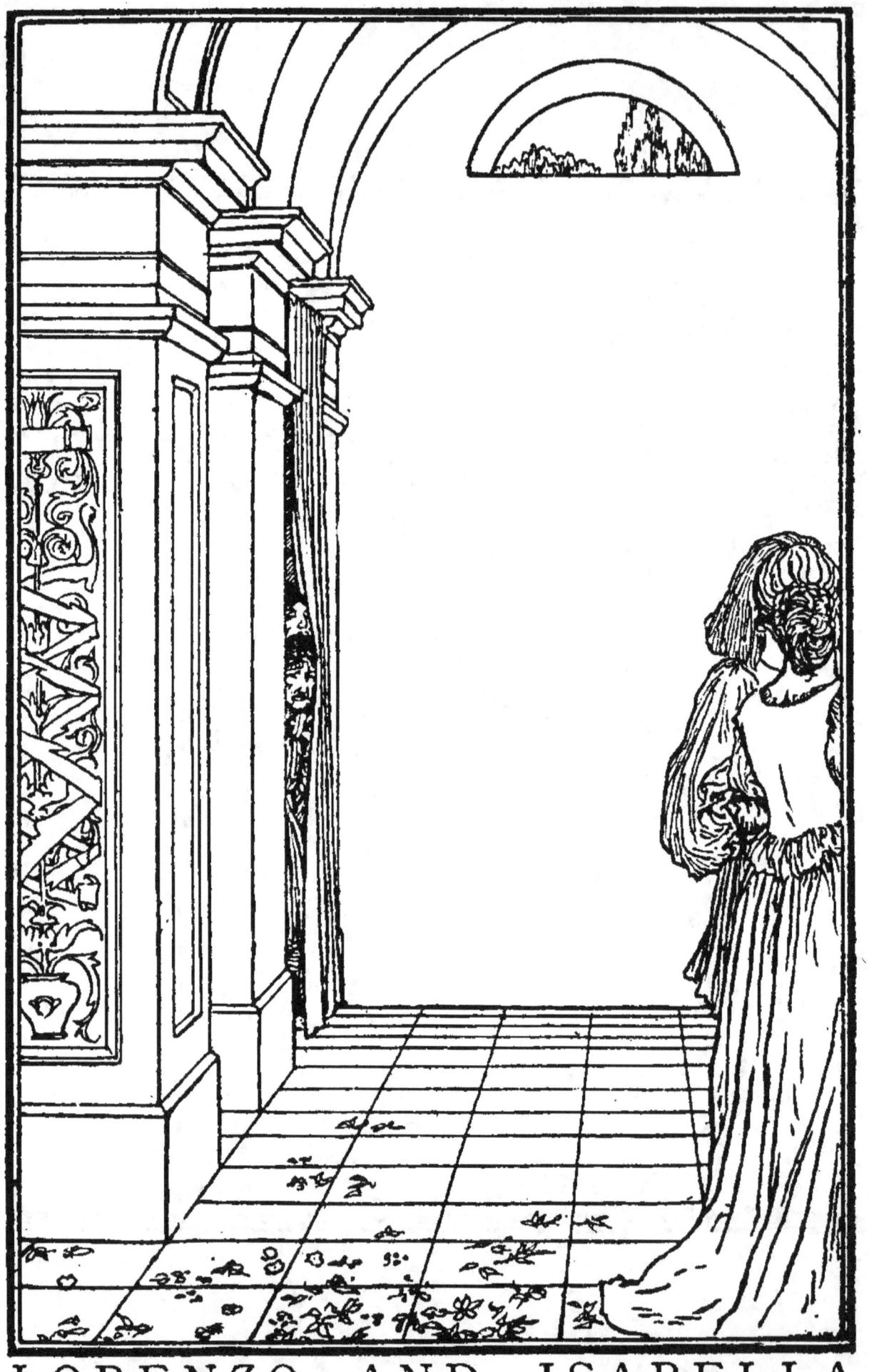

LORENZO AND ISABELLA

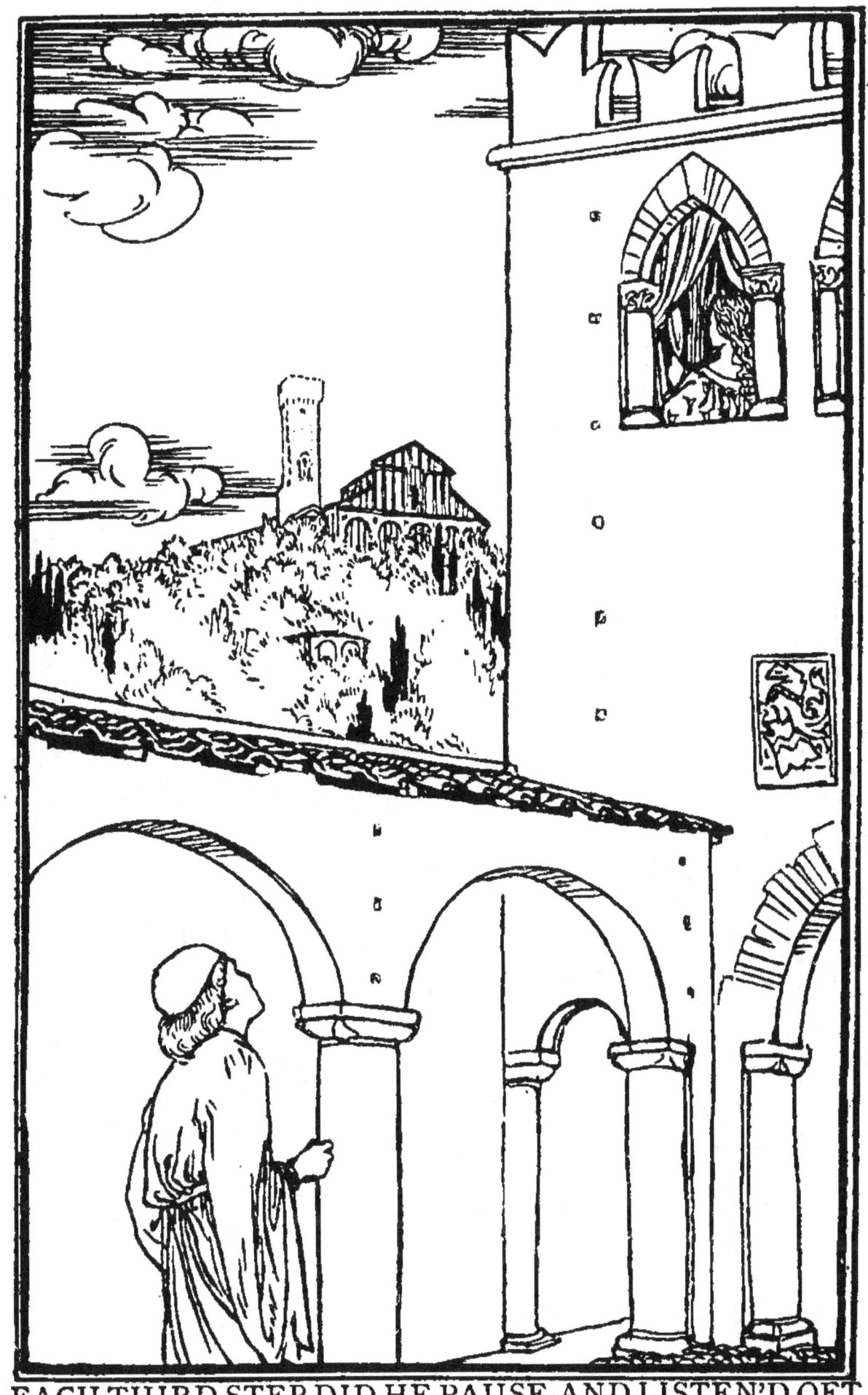
EACH THIRD STEP DID HE PAUSE, AND LISTEN'D OFT
IF HE COULD HEAR HIS LADY'S MATIN-SONG

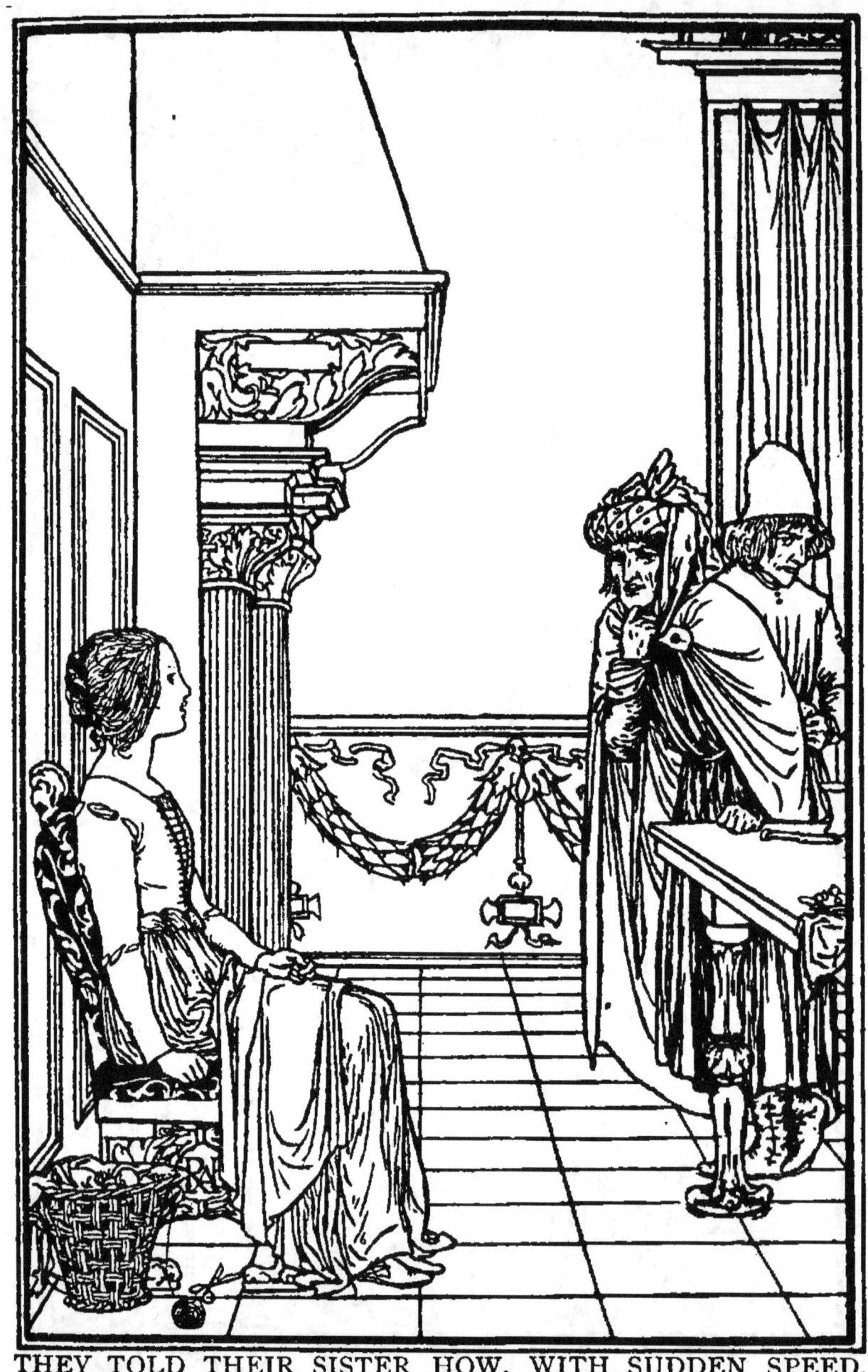

THEY TOLD THEIR SISTER HOW, WITH SUDDEN SPEED,
LORENZO HAD TA'EN SHIP FOR FOREIGN LANDS

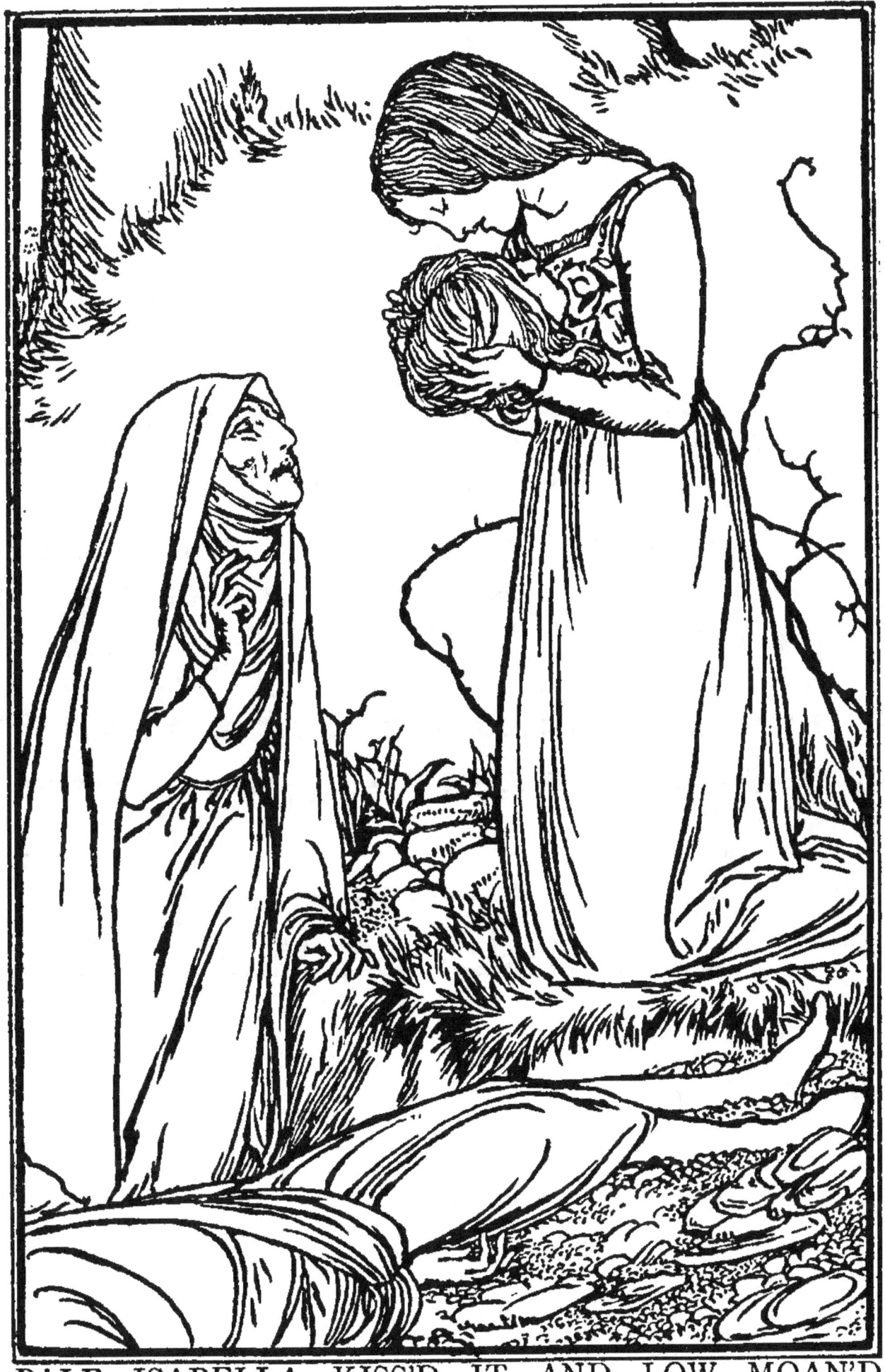

PALE ISABELLA KISS'D IT AND LOW MOAN'D

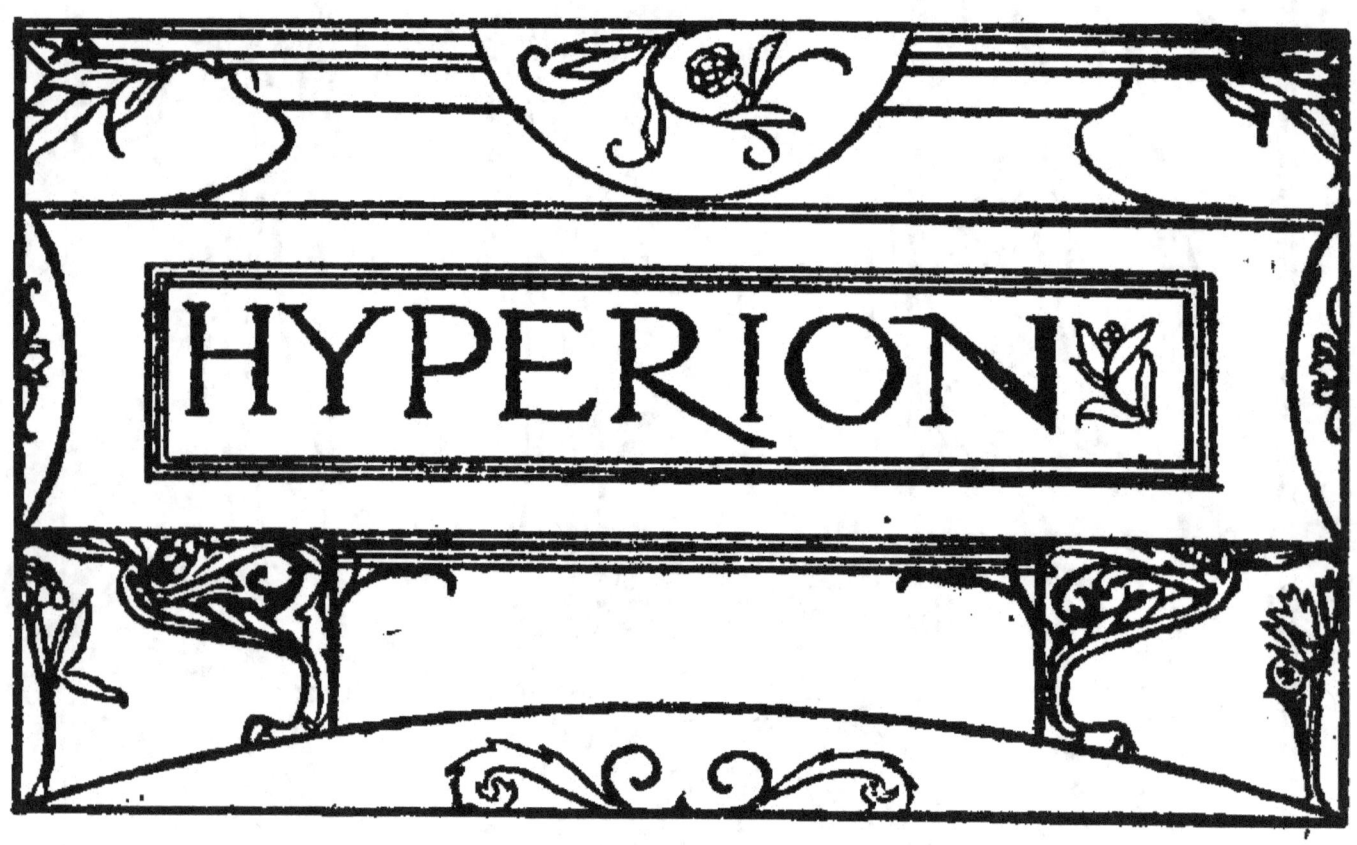

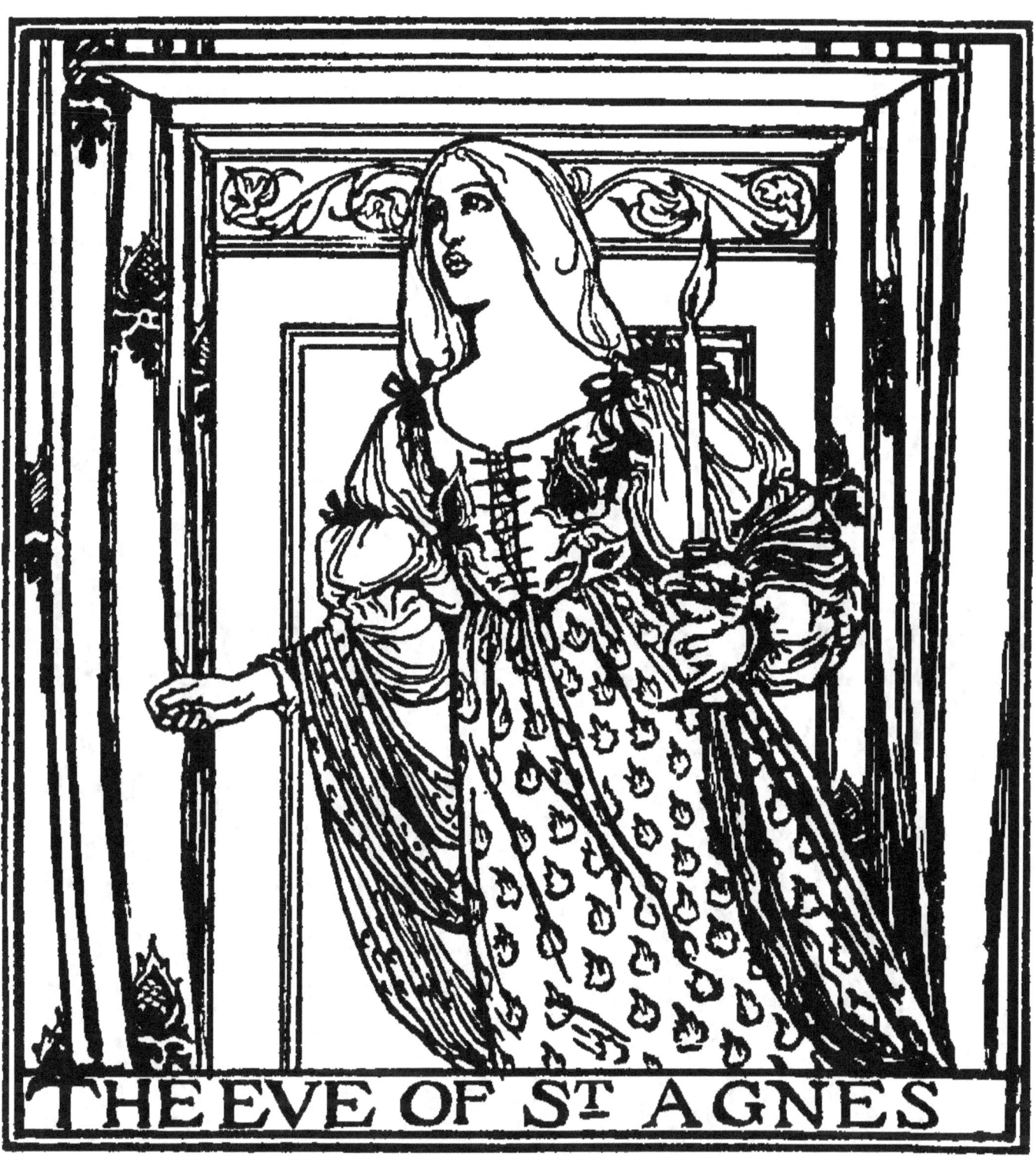

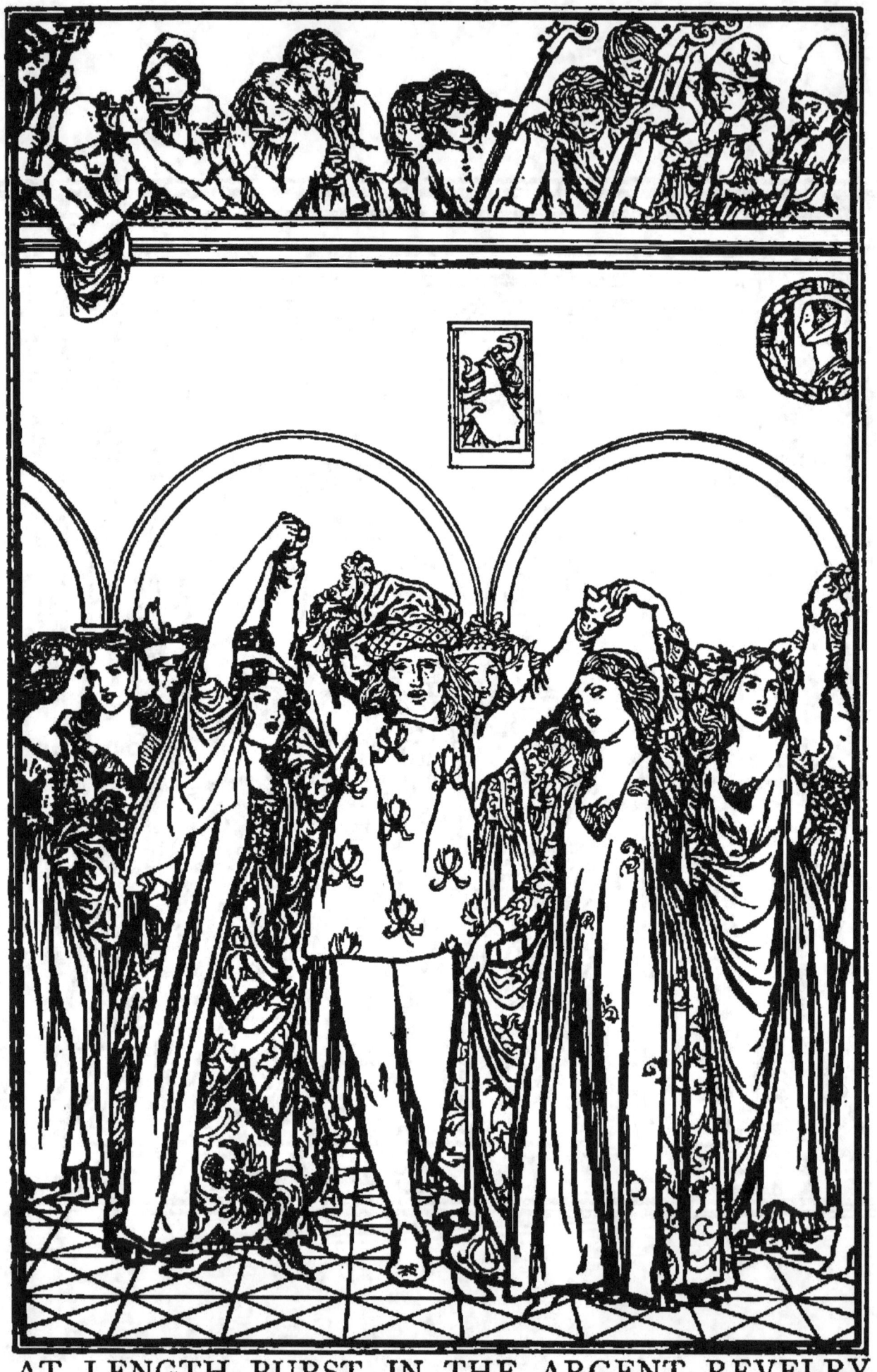

AT LENGTH BURST IN THE ARGENT REVELRY

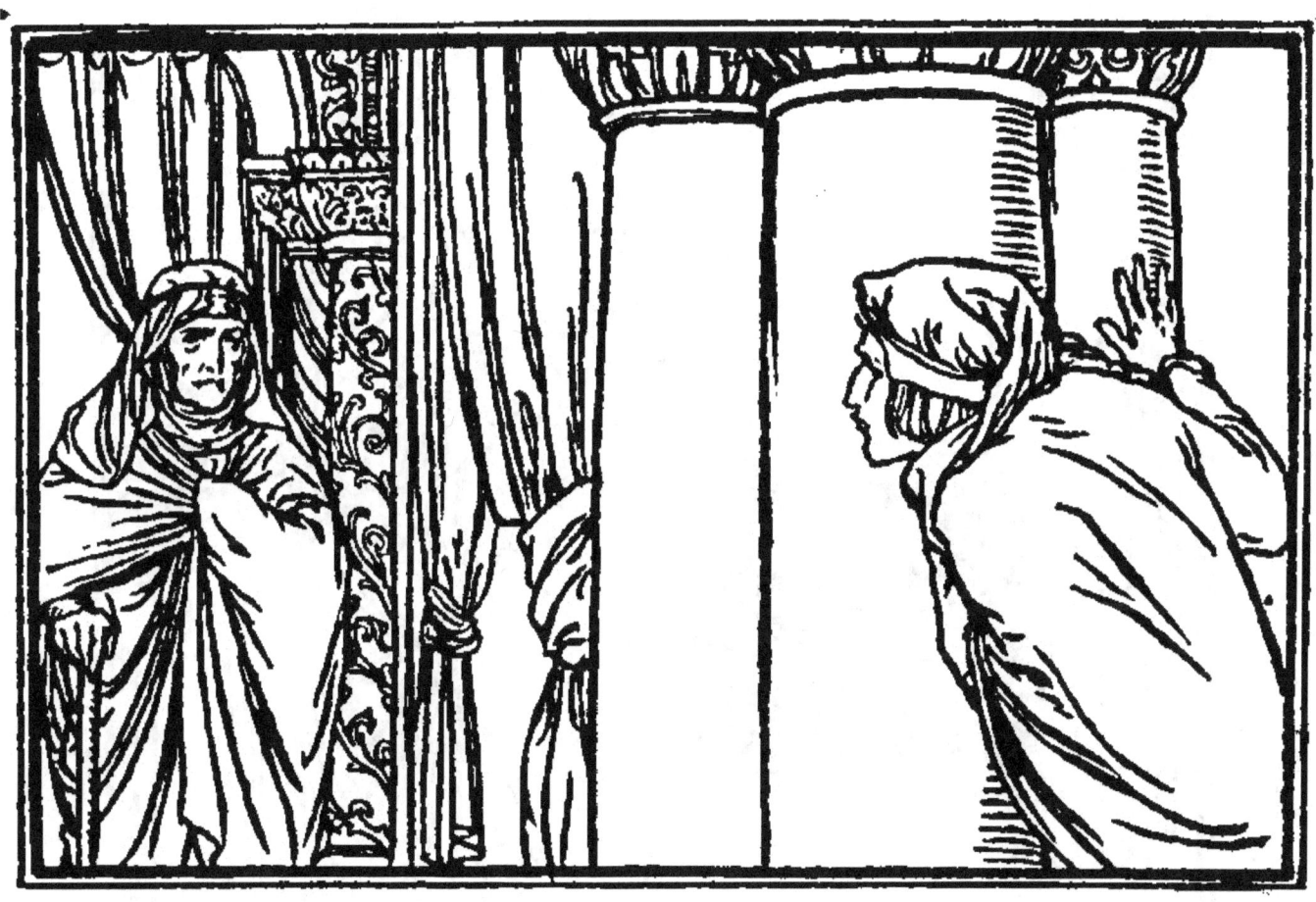

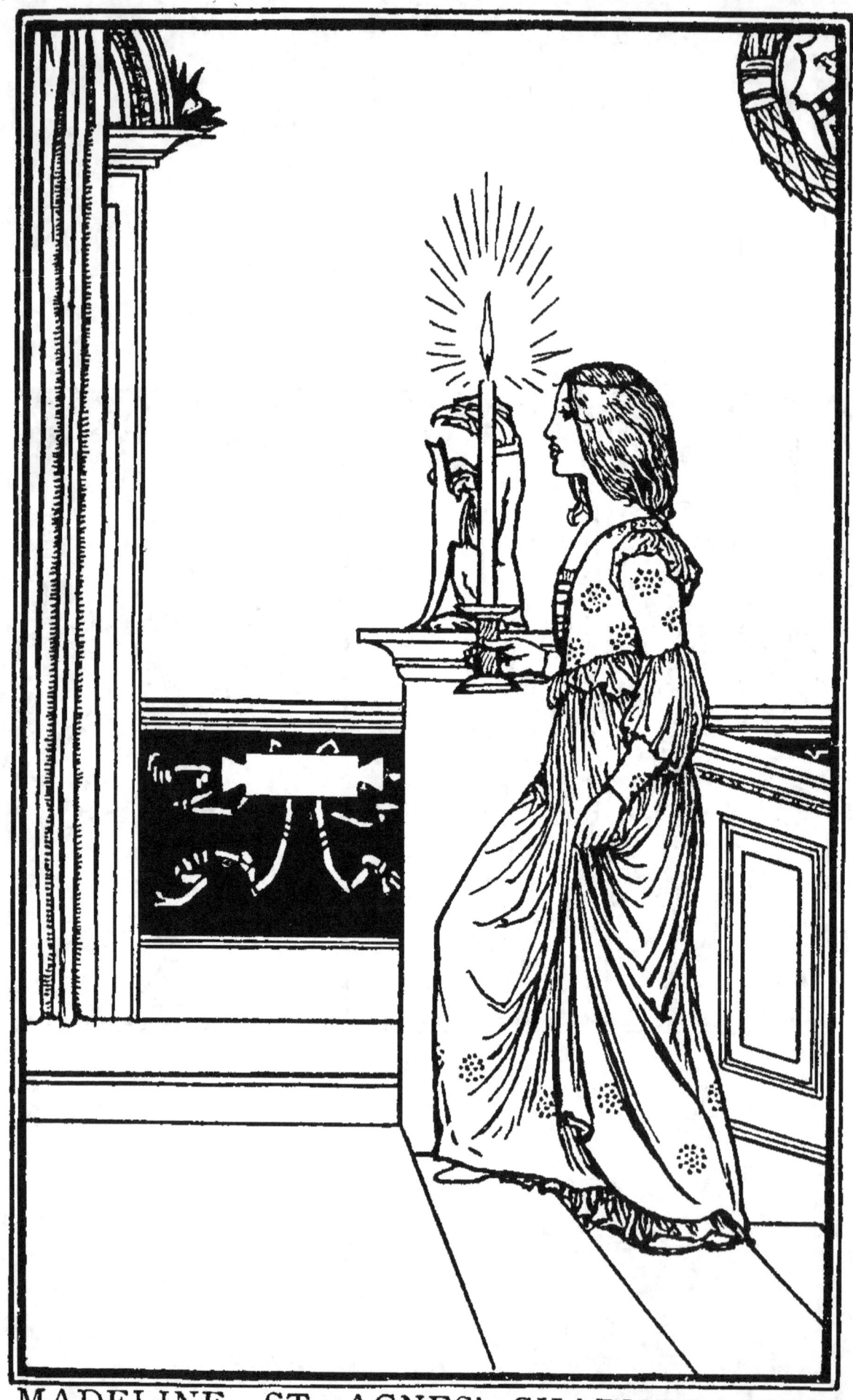

MADELINE, ST. AGNES' CHARMED MAID

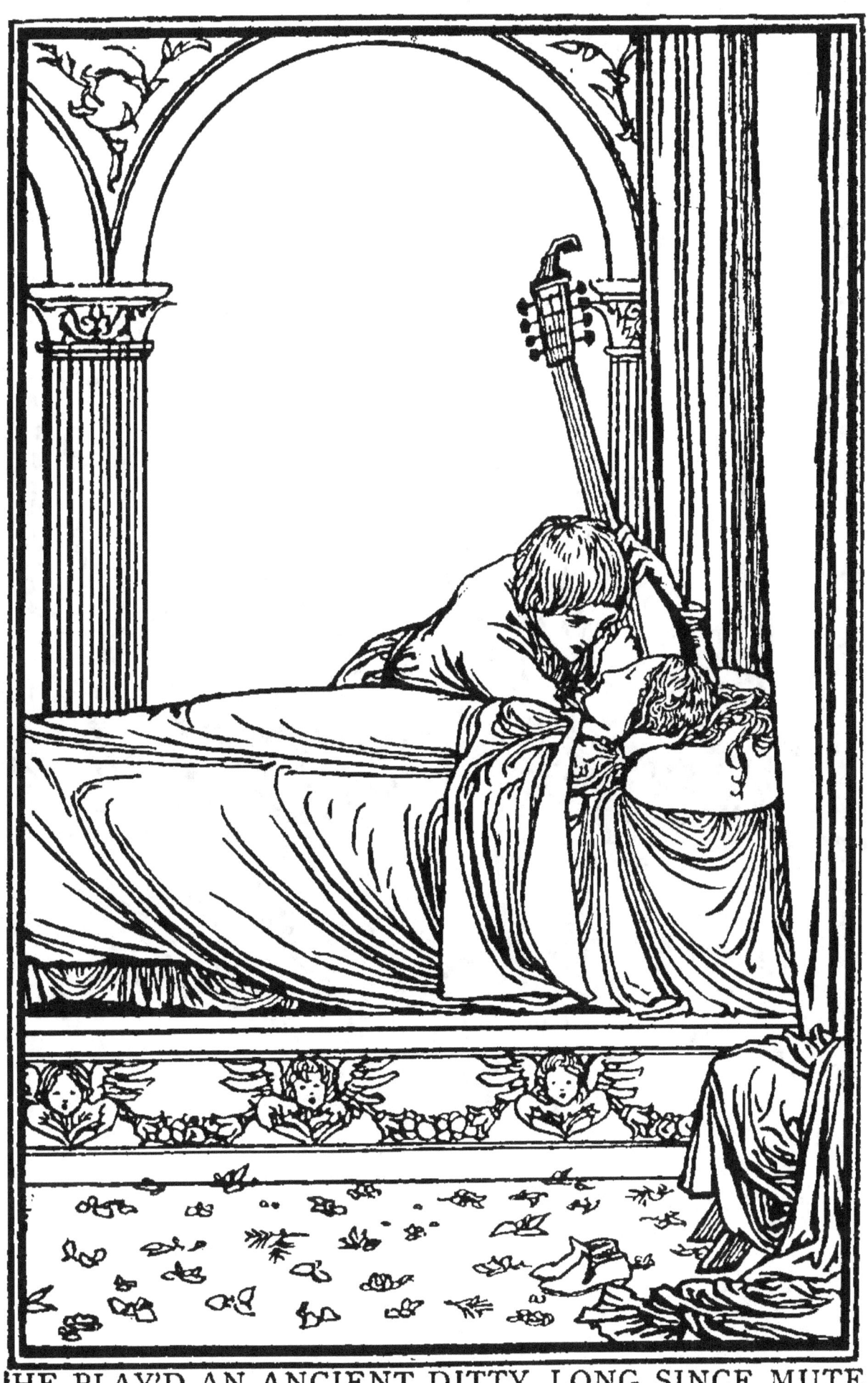

HE PLAY'D AN ANCIENT DITTY, LONG SINCE MUTE
CLOSE TO HER EAR TOUCHING THE MELODY

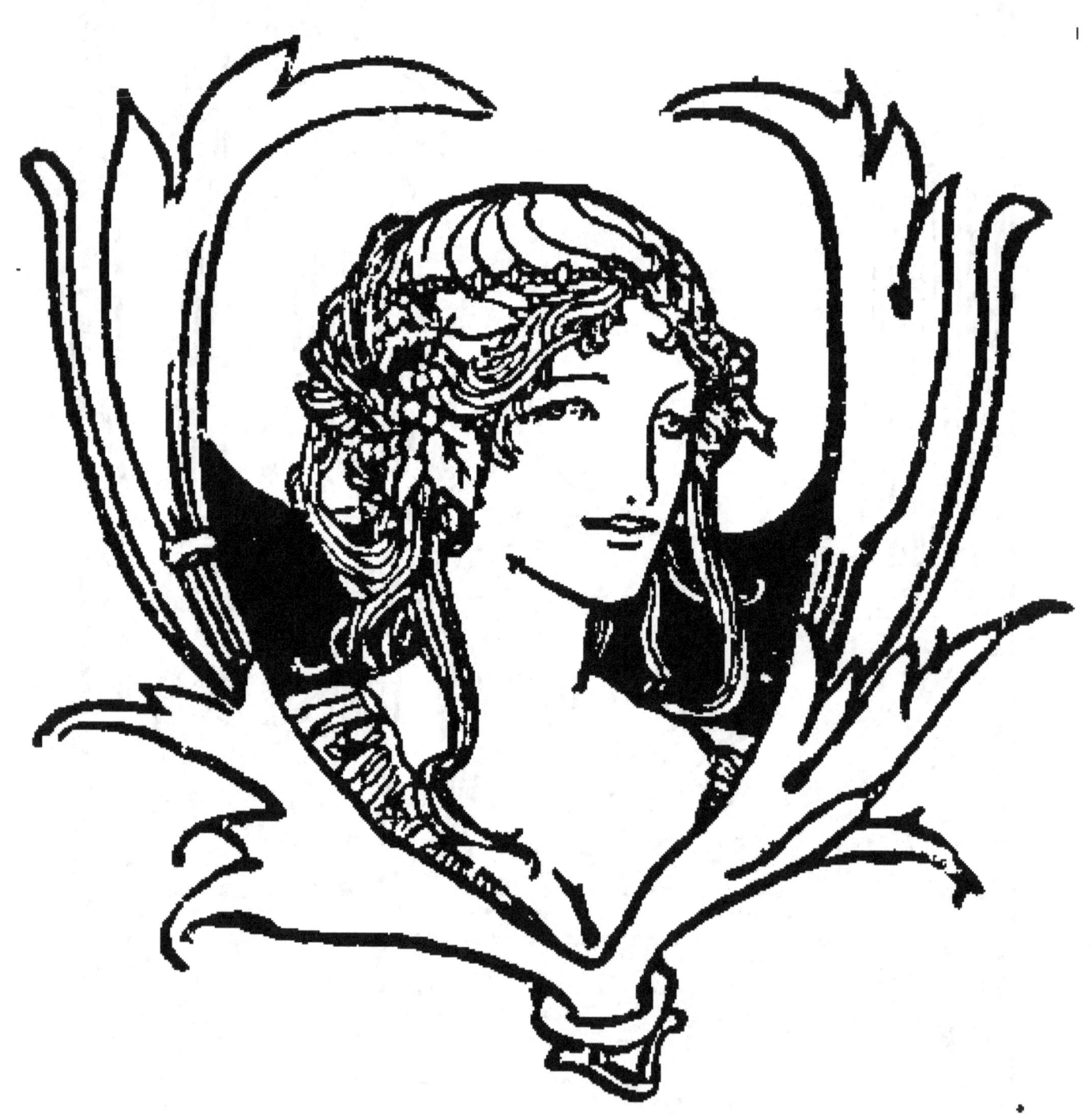

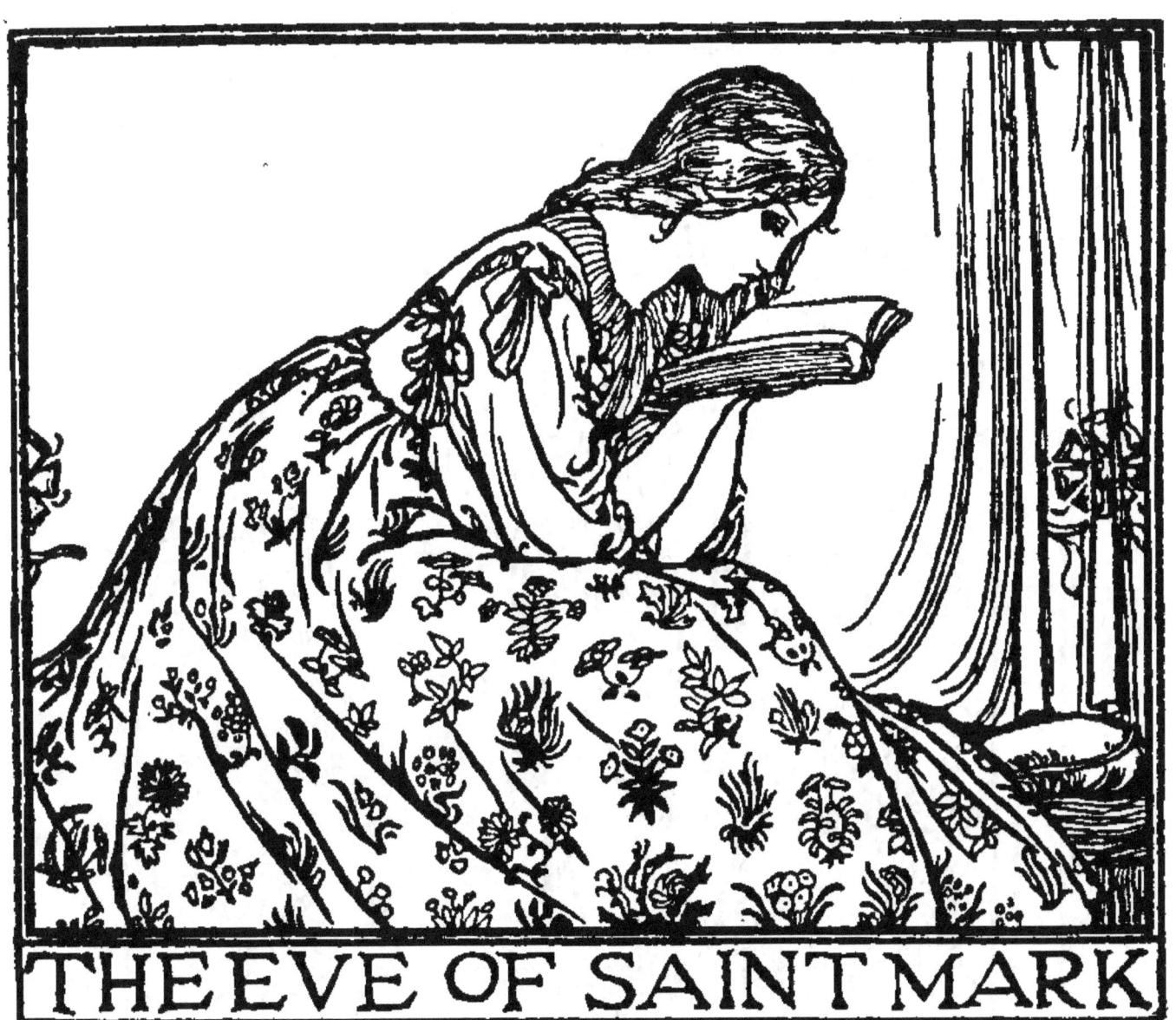

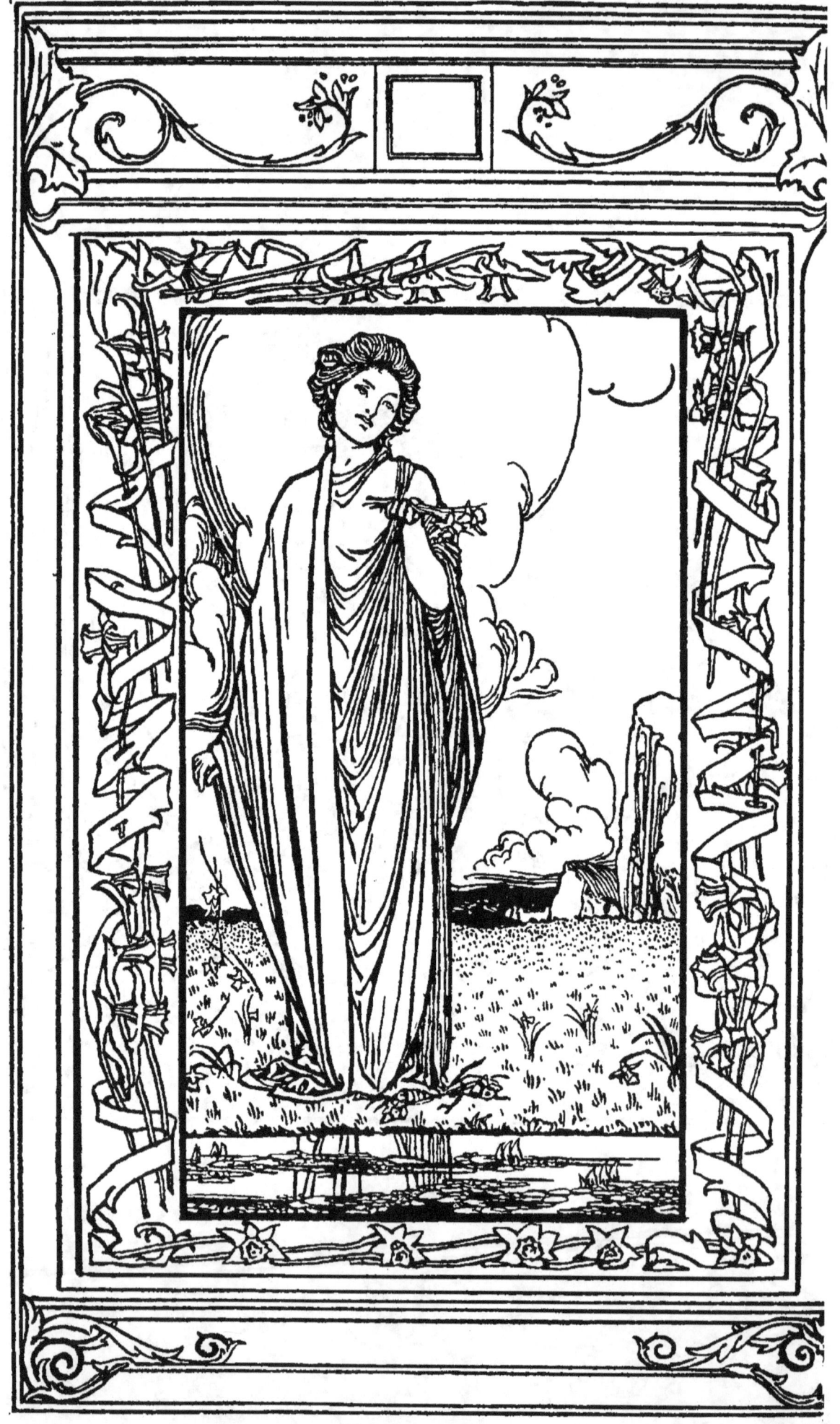

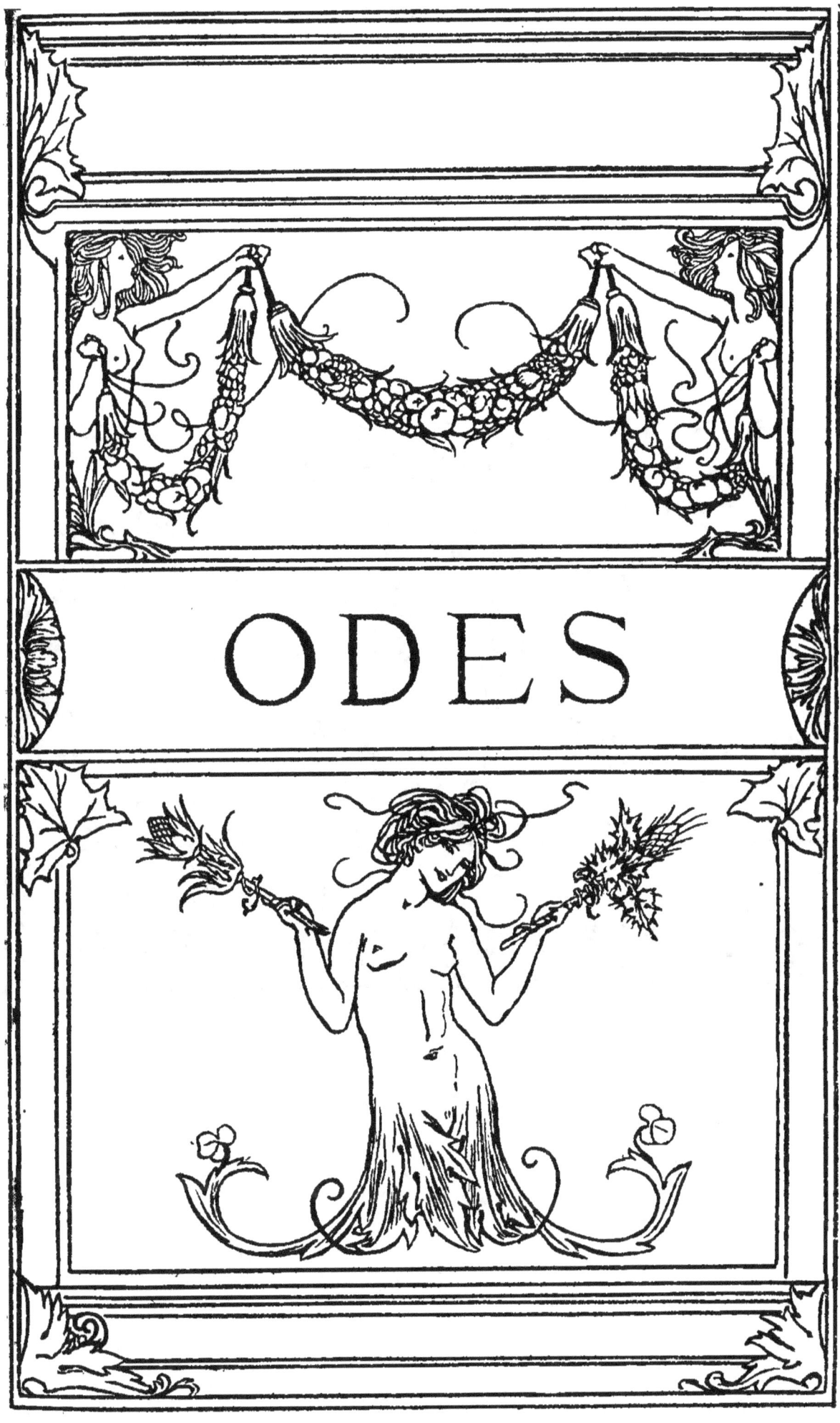

ODES

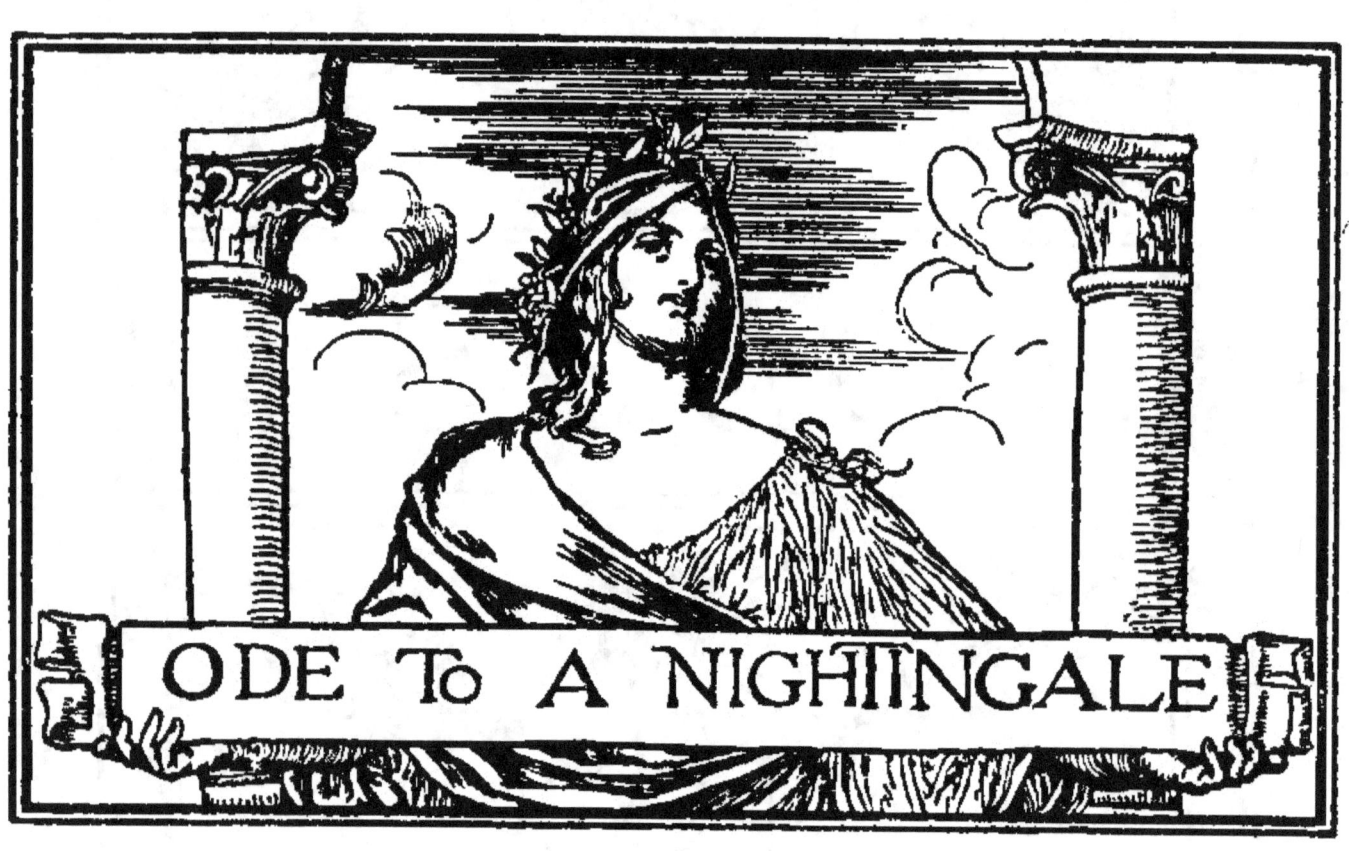

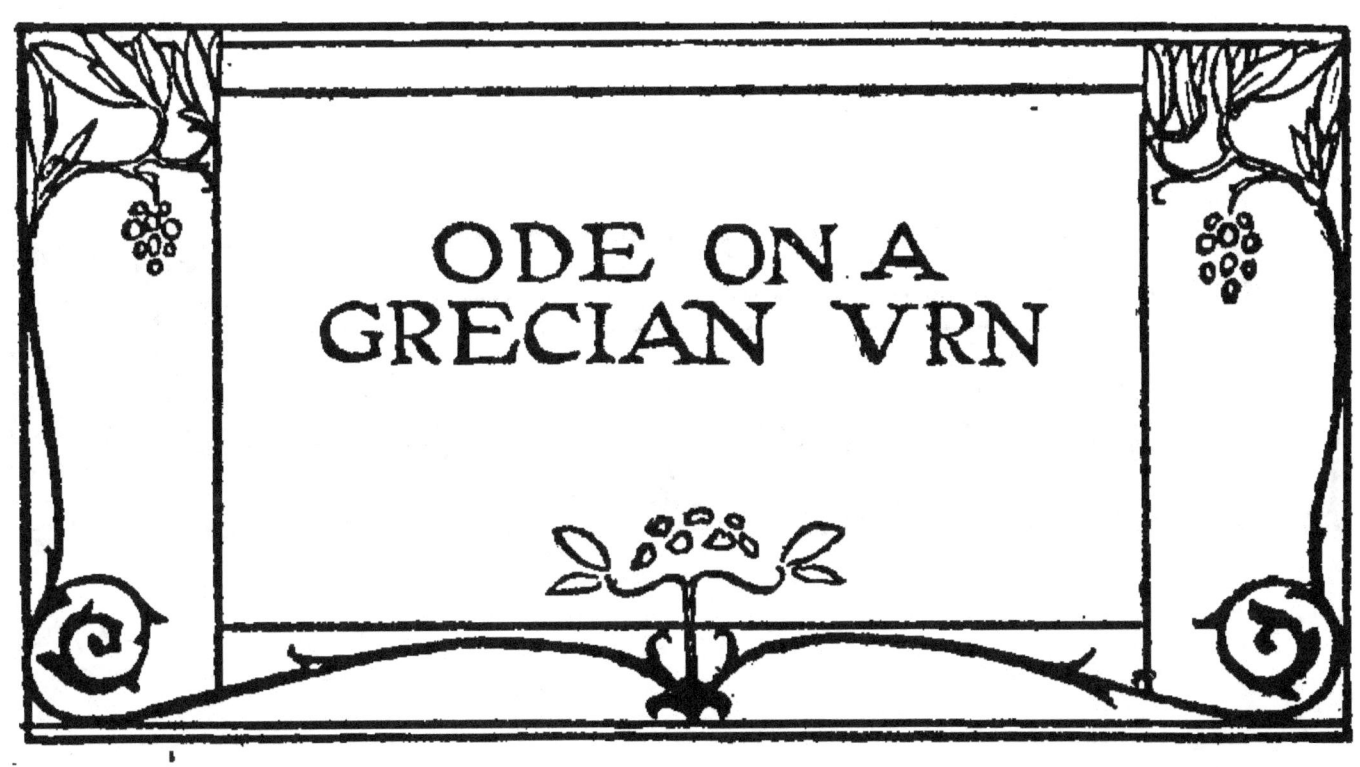

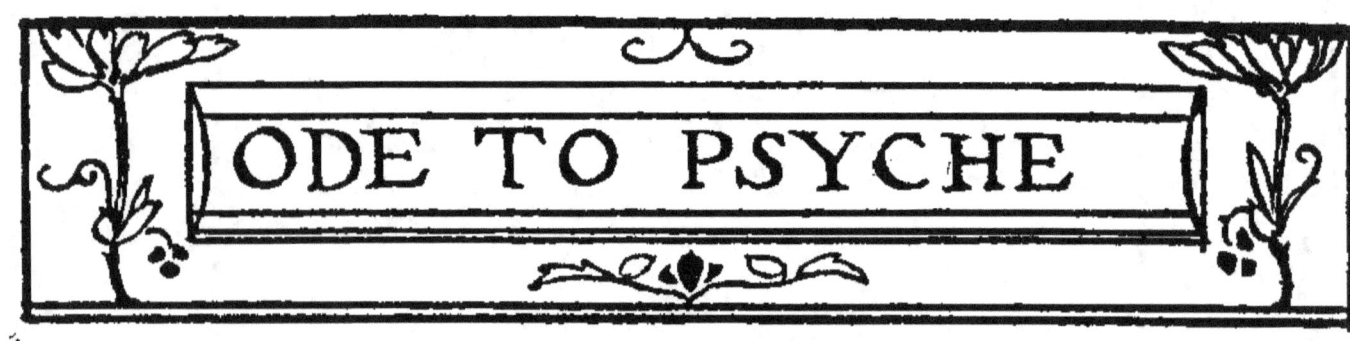

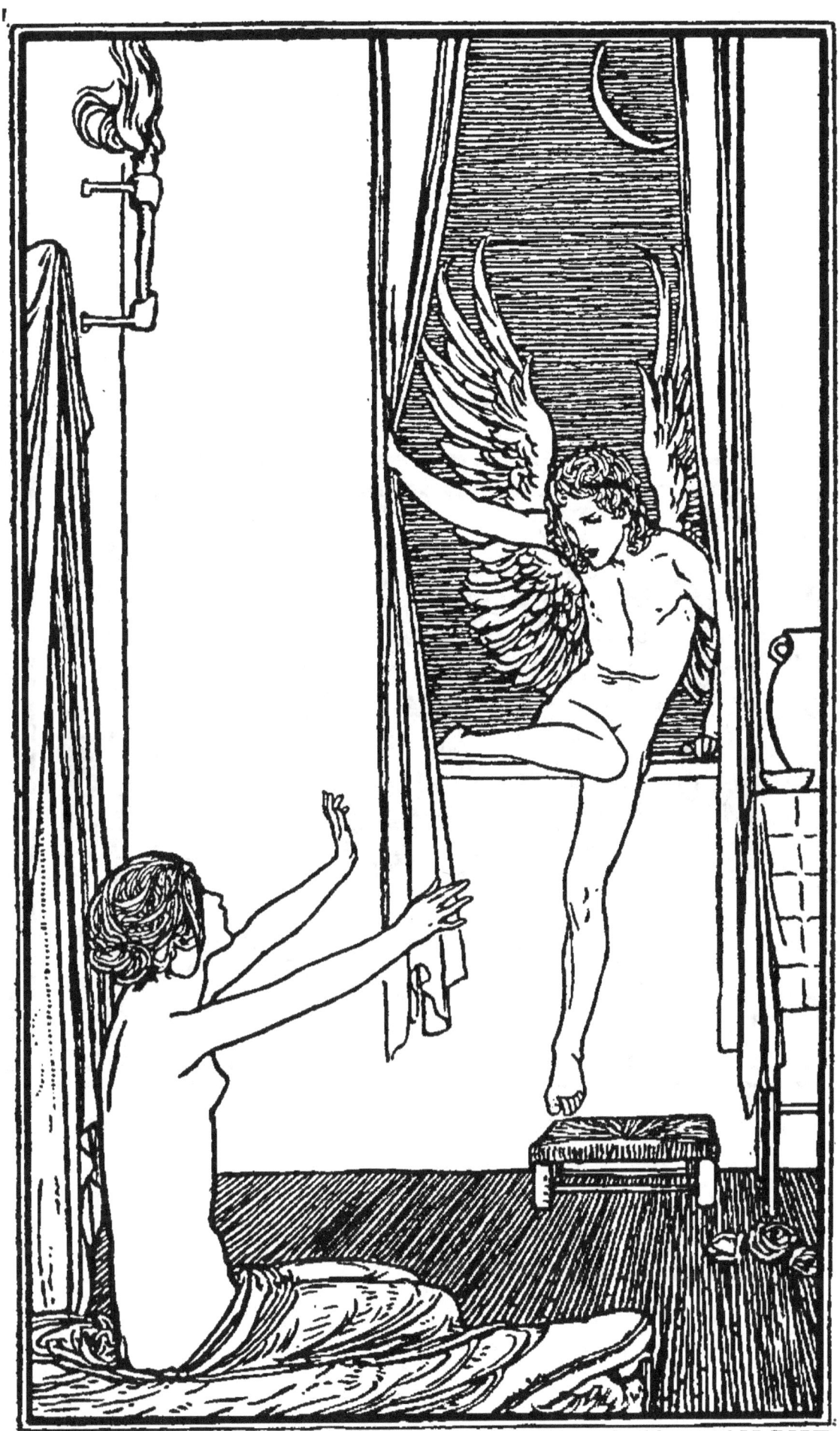

A BRIGHT TORCH, AND A CASEMENT OPE AT NIGHT
TO LET THE WARM LOVE IN!

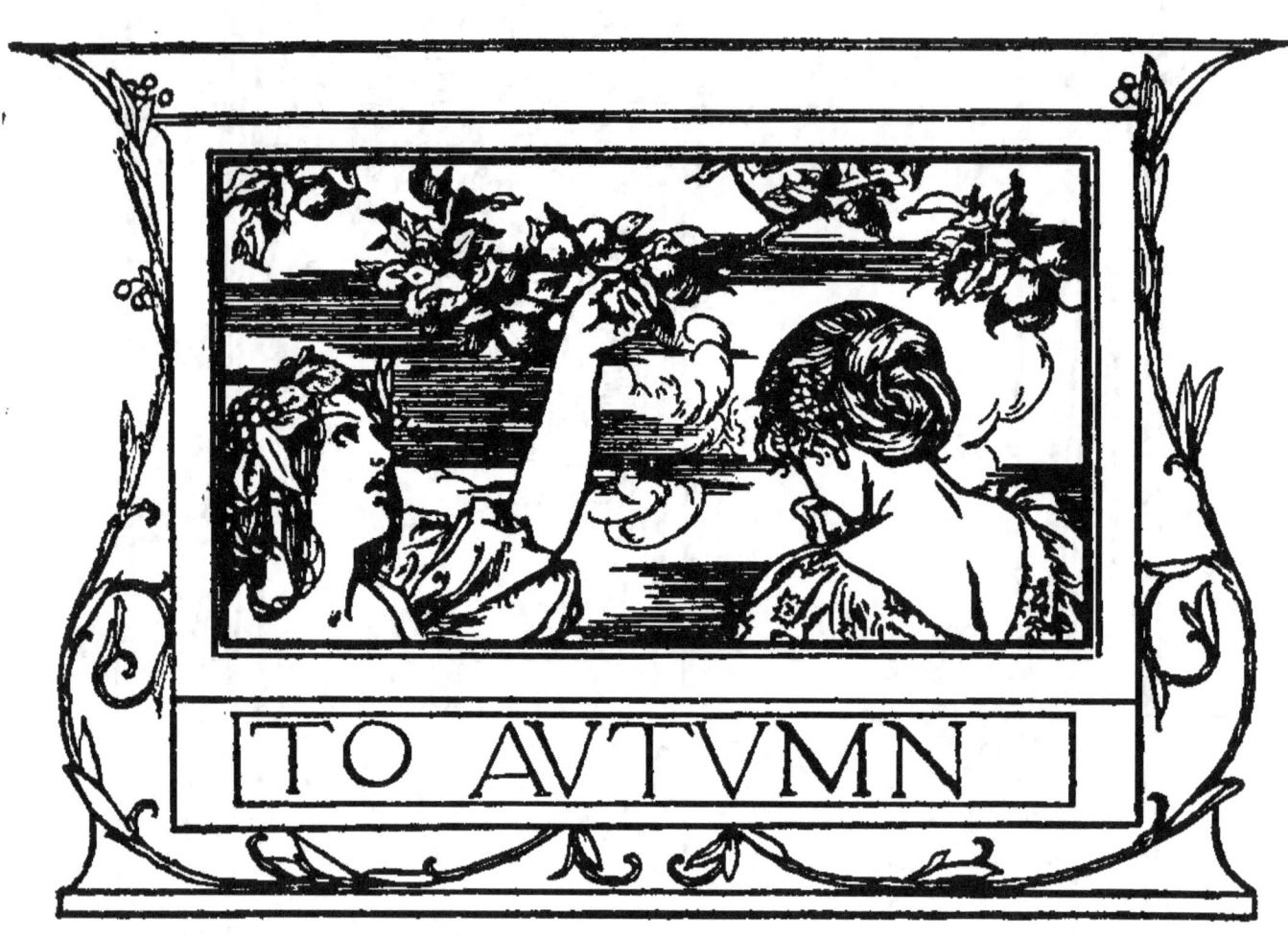

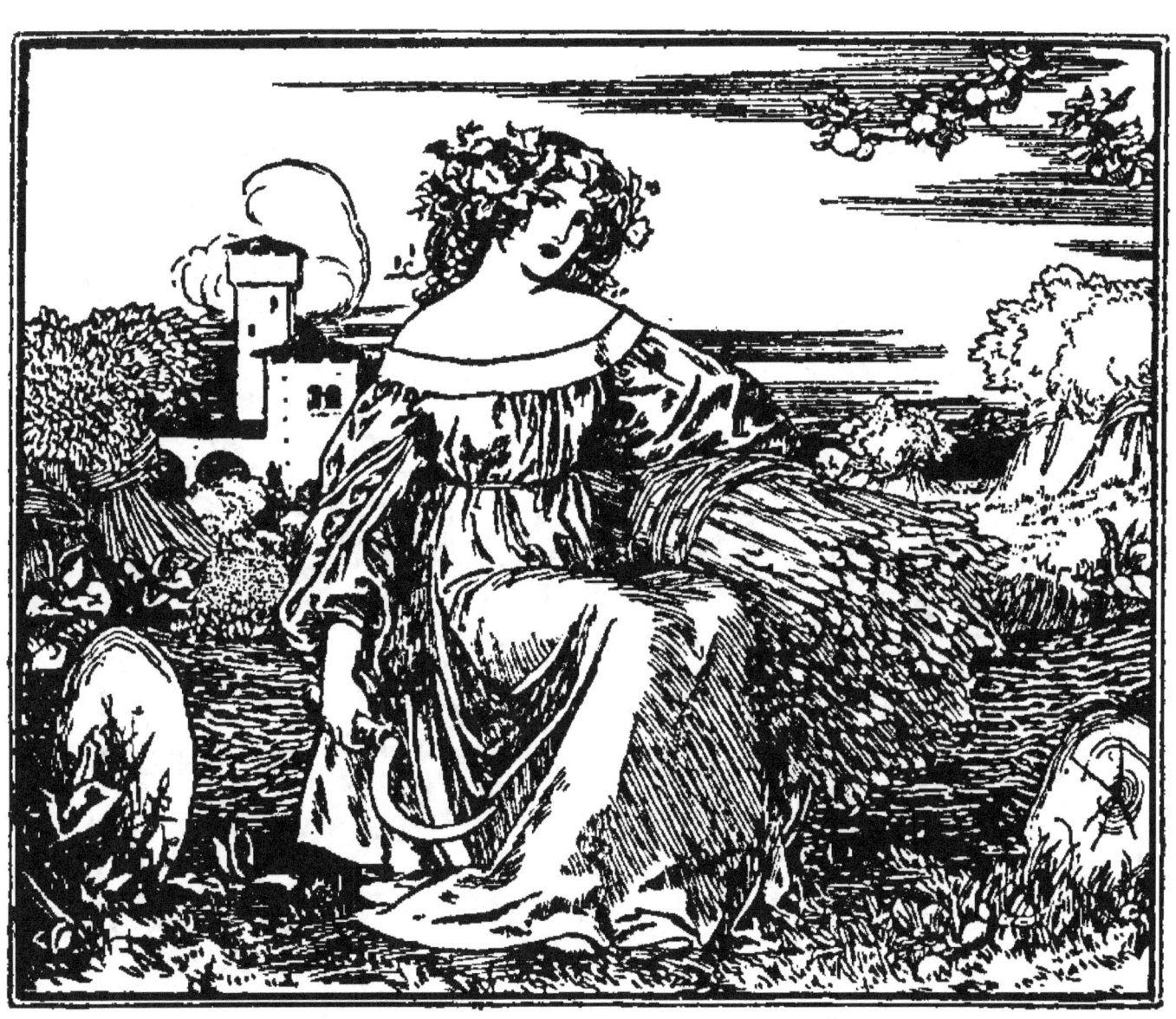

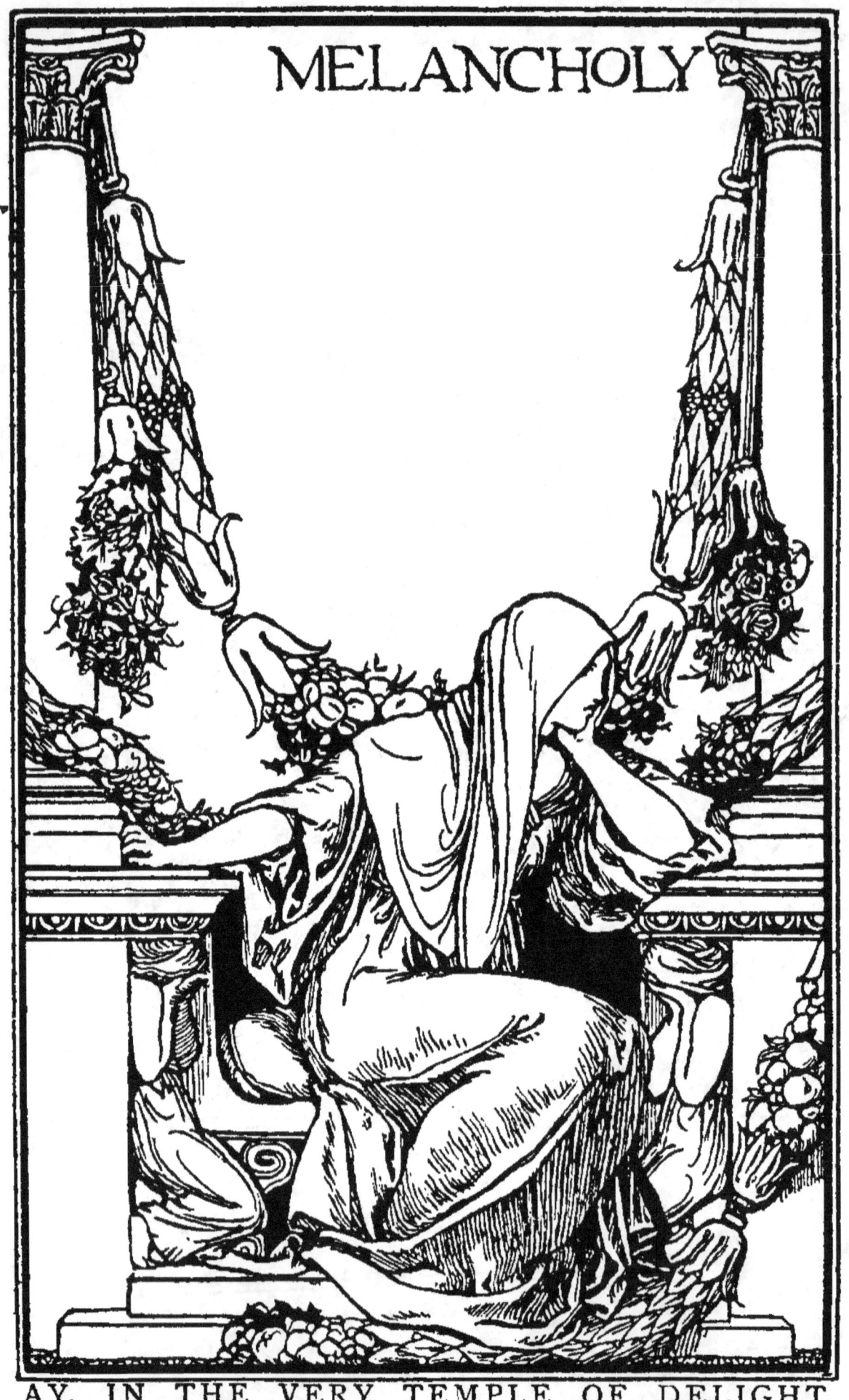

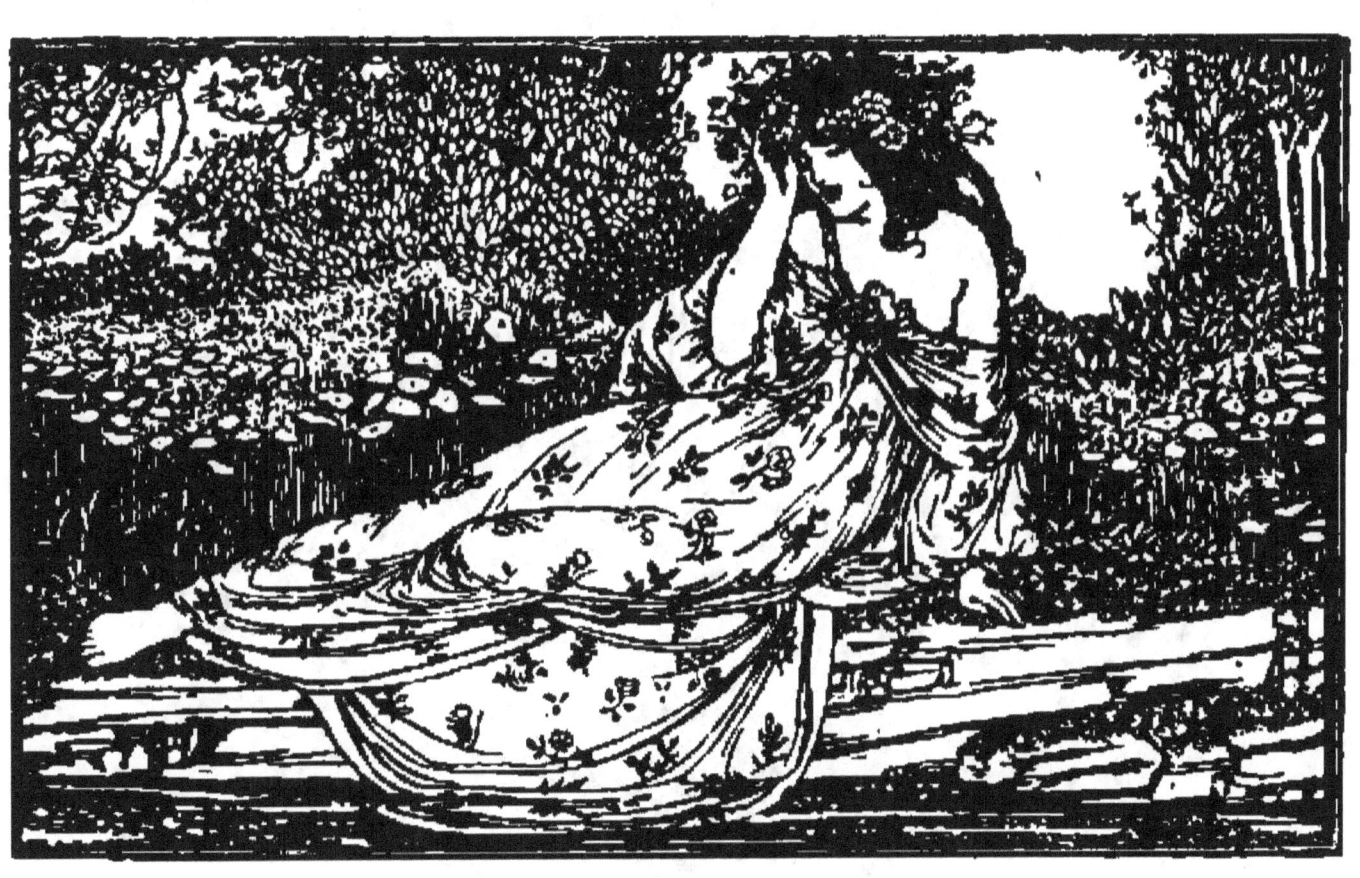

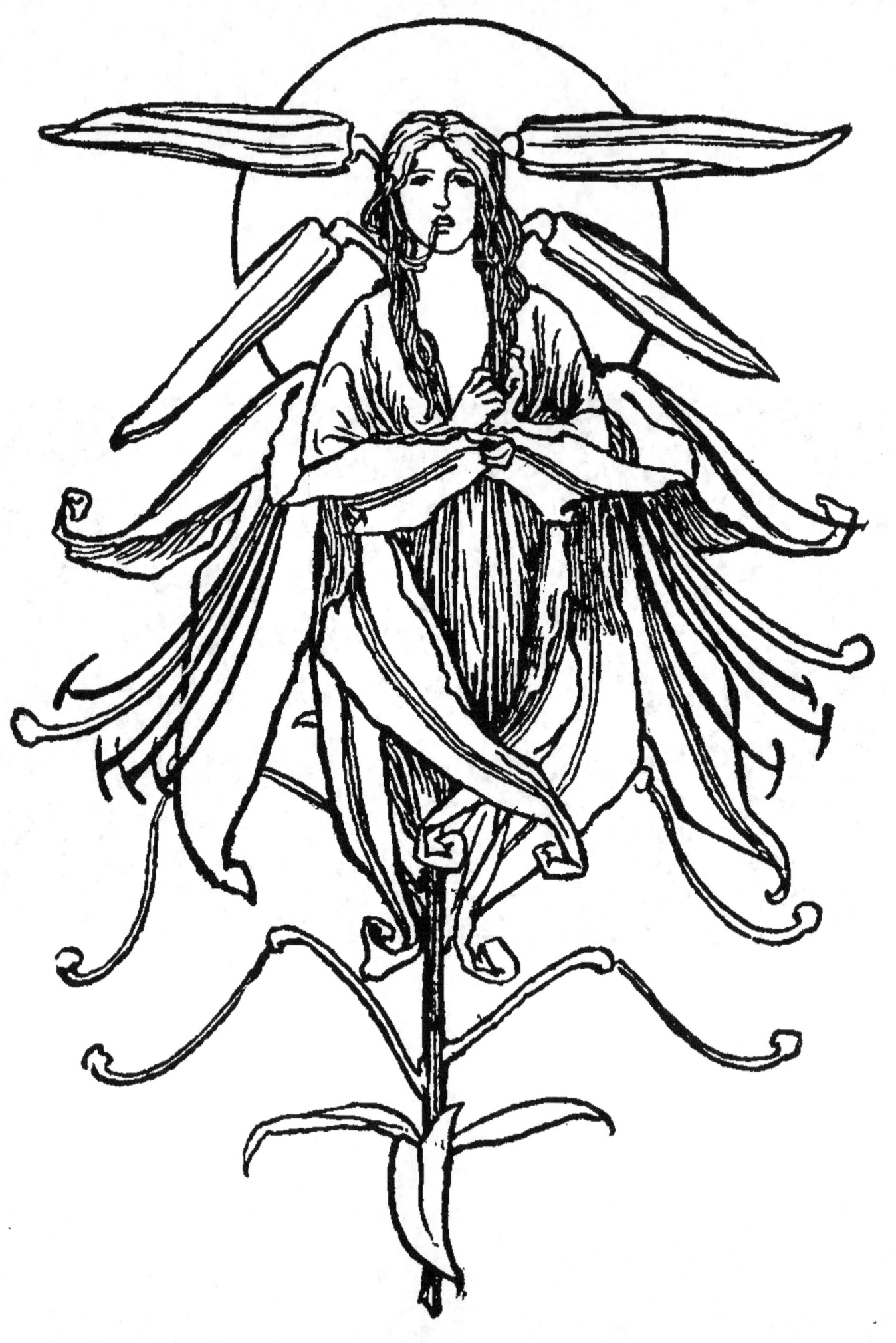

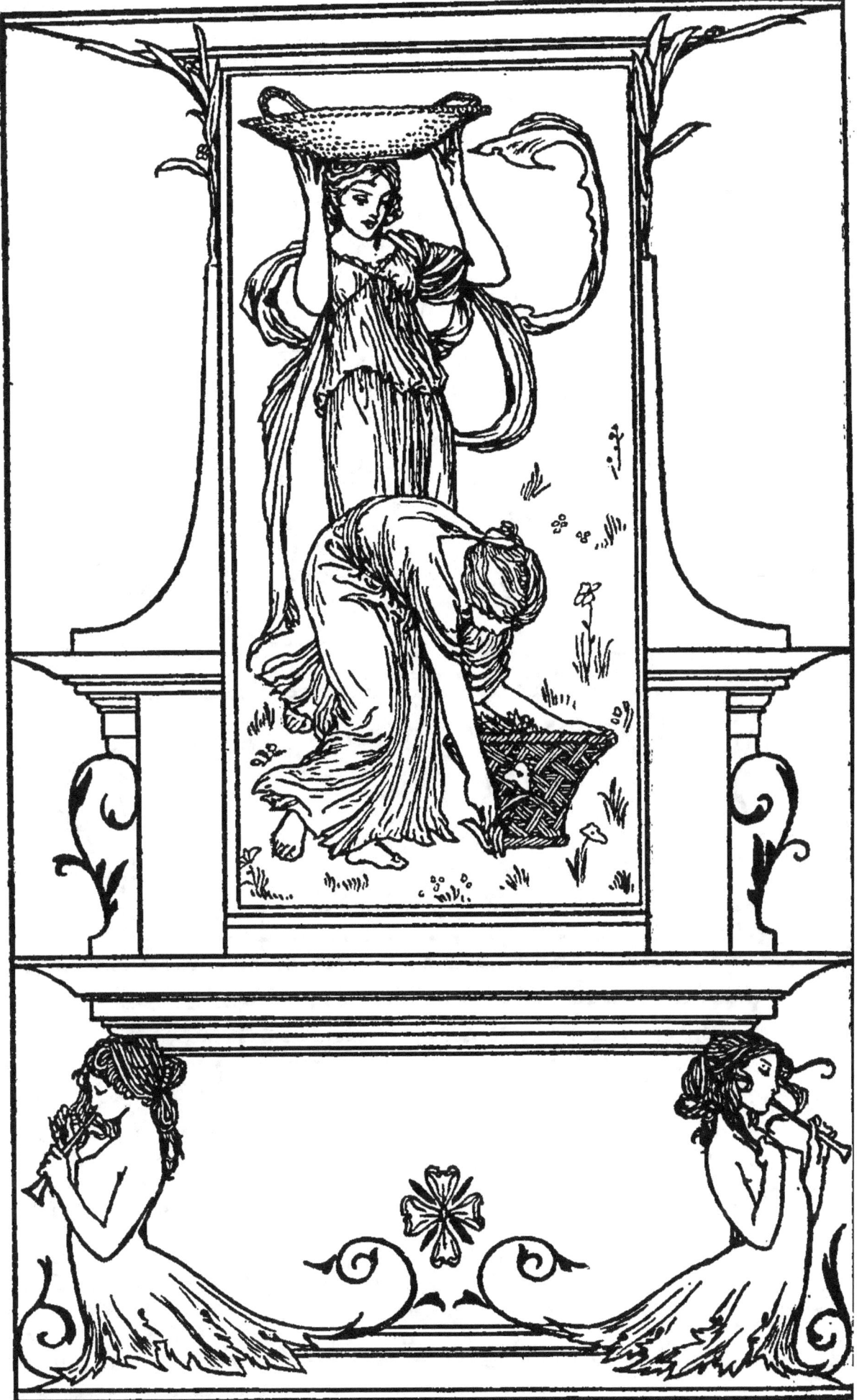

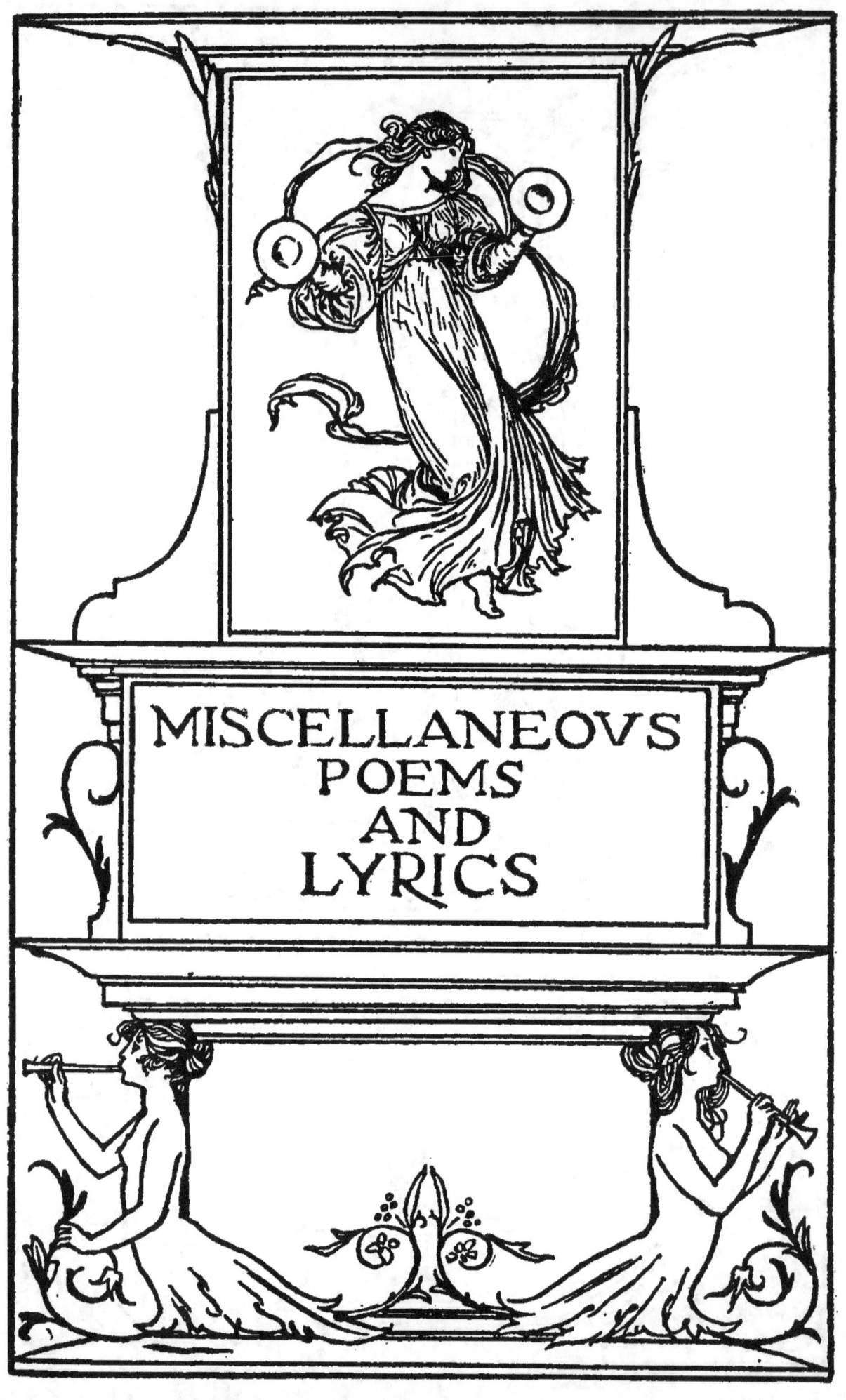

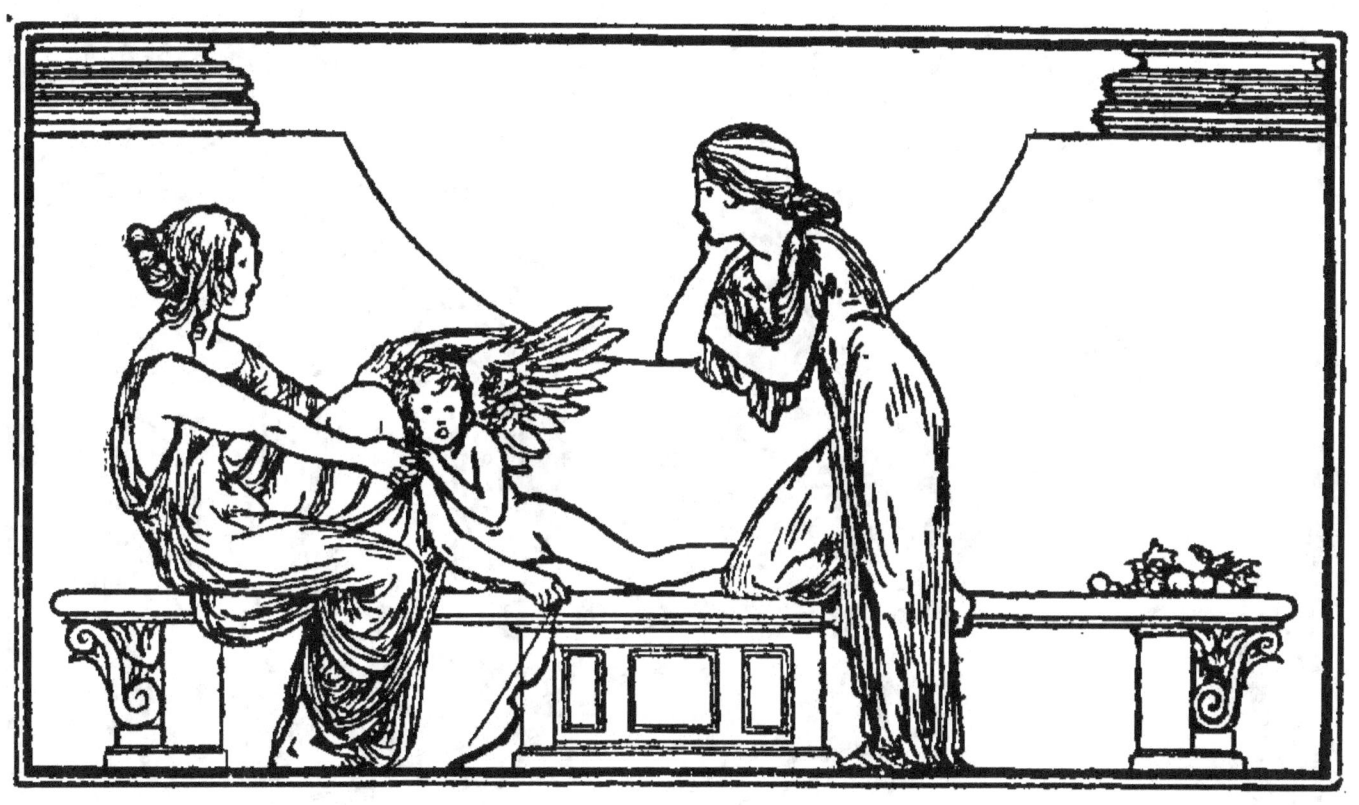

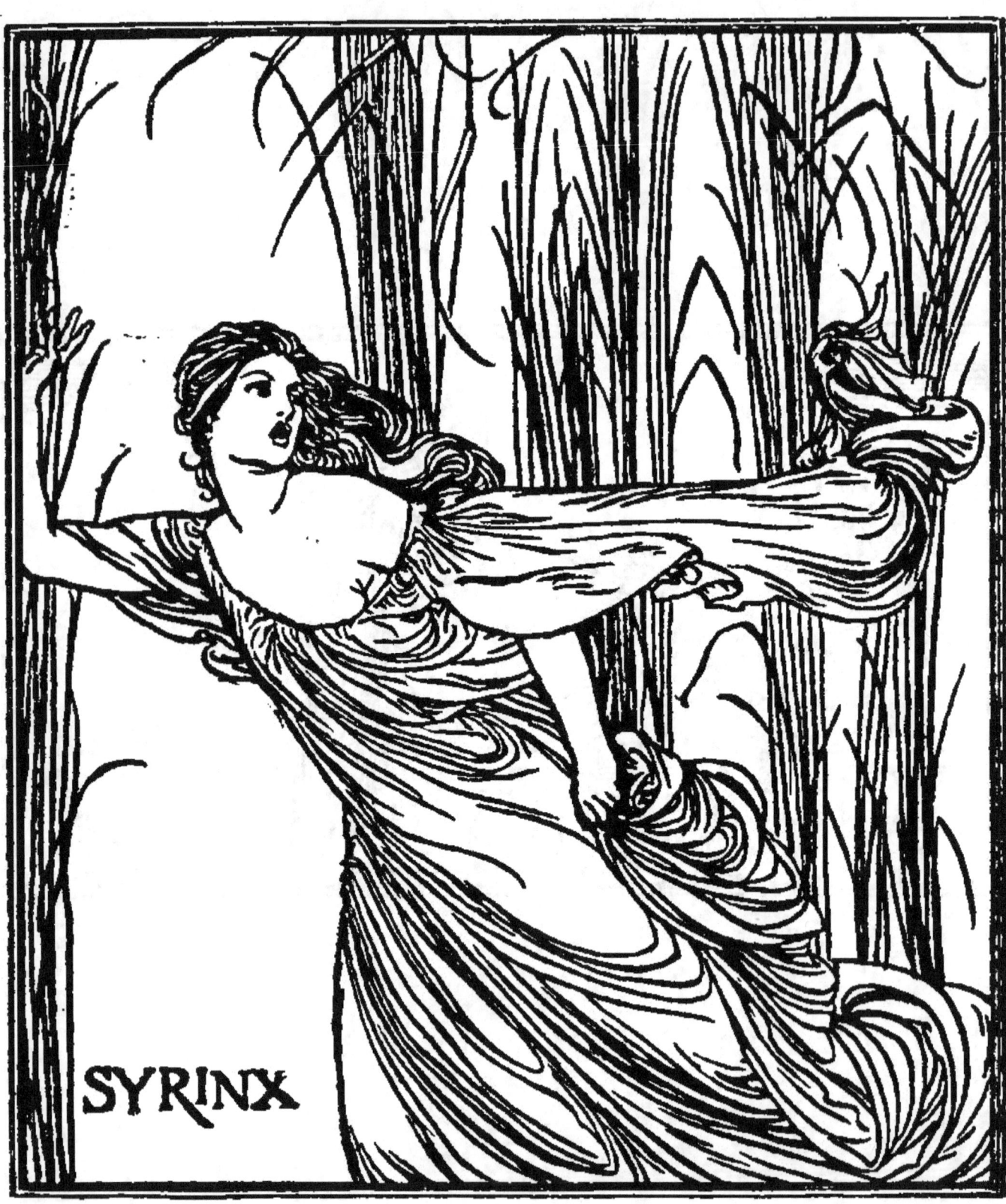

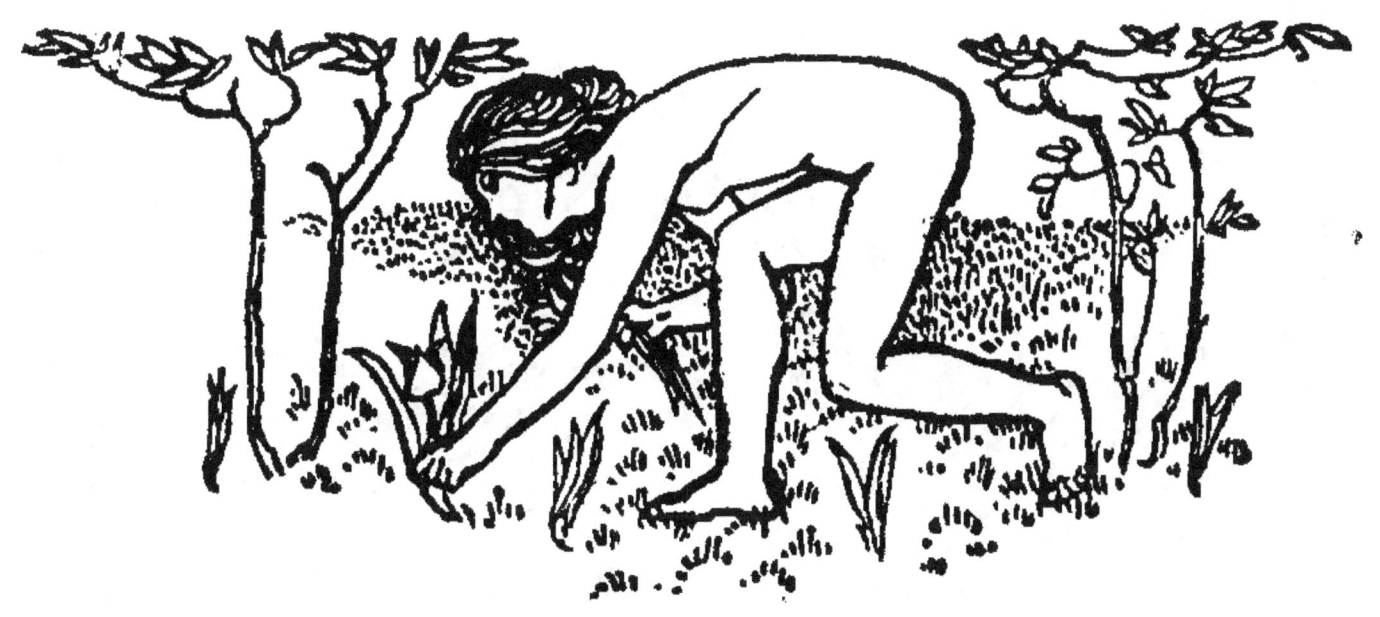

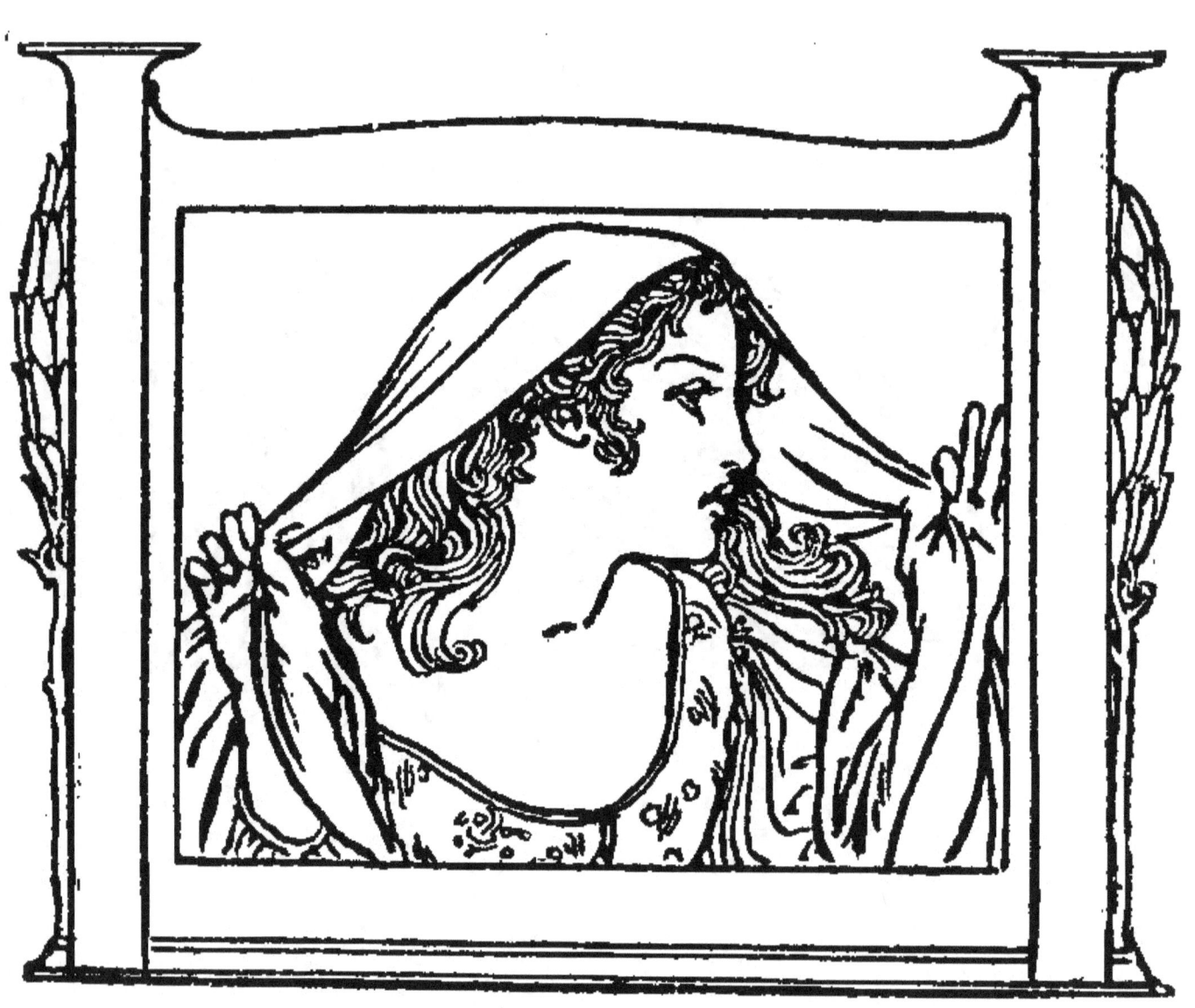

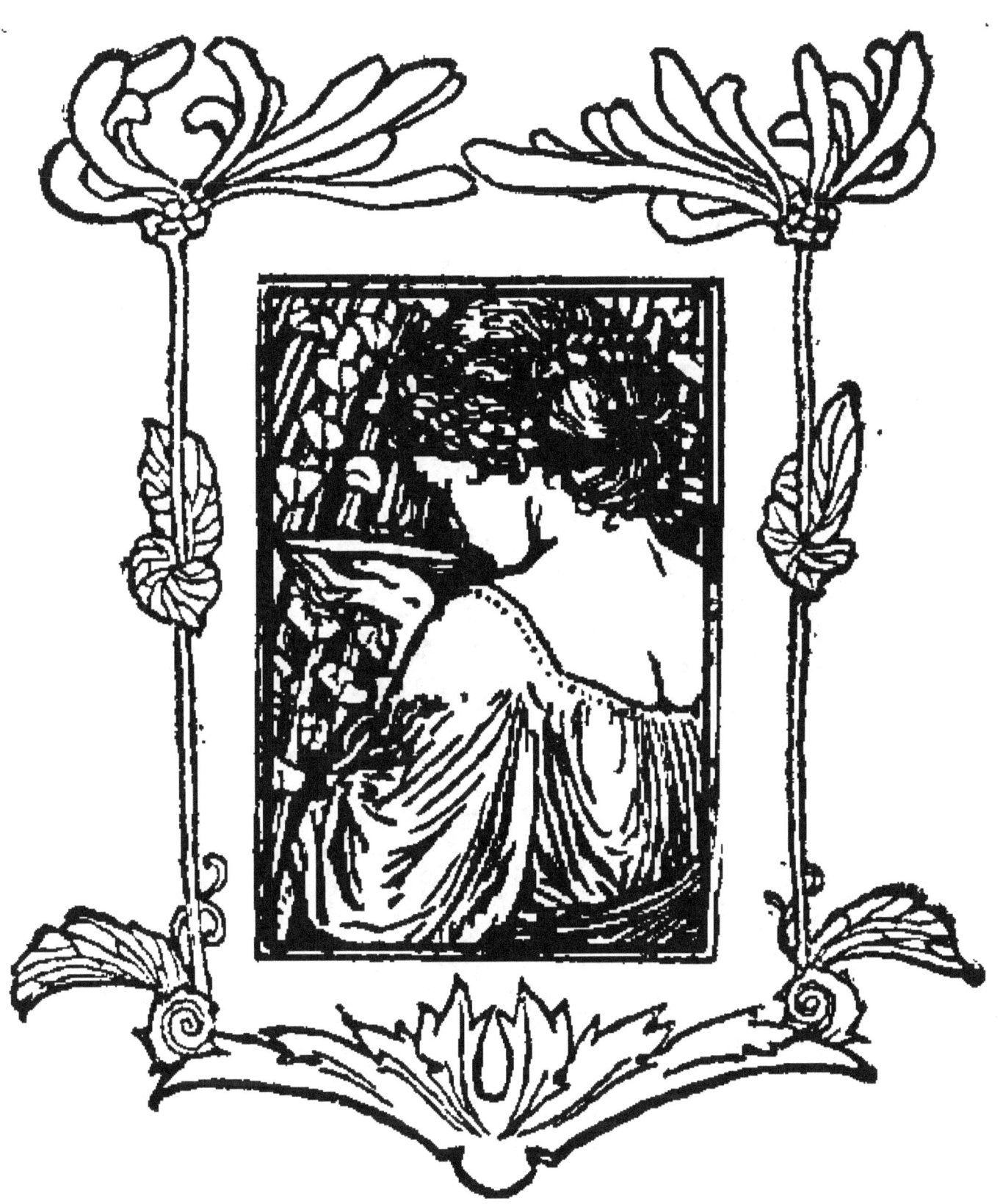

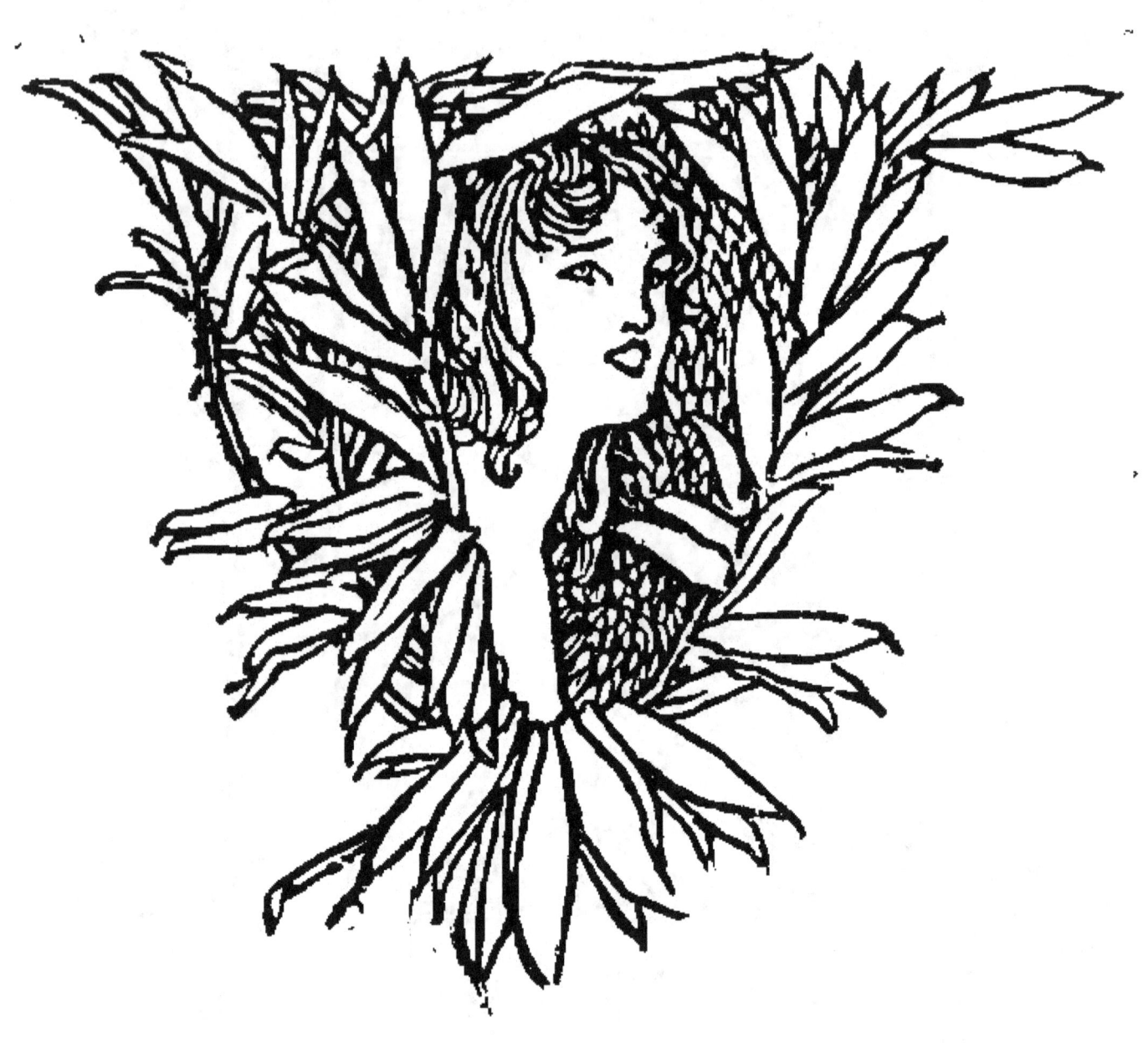

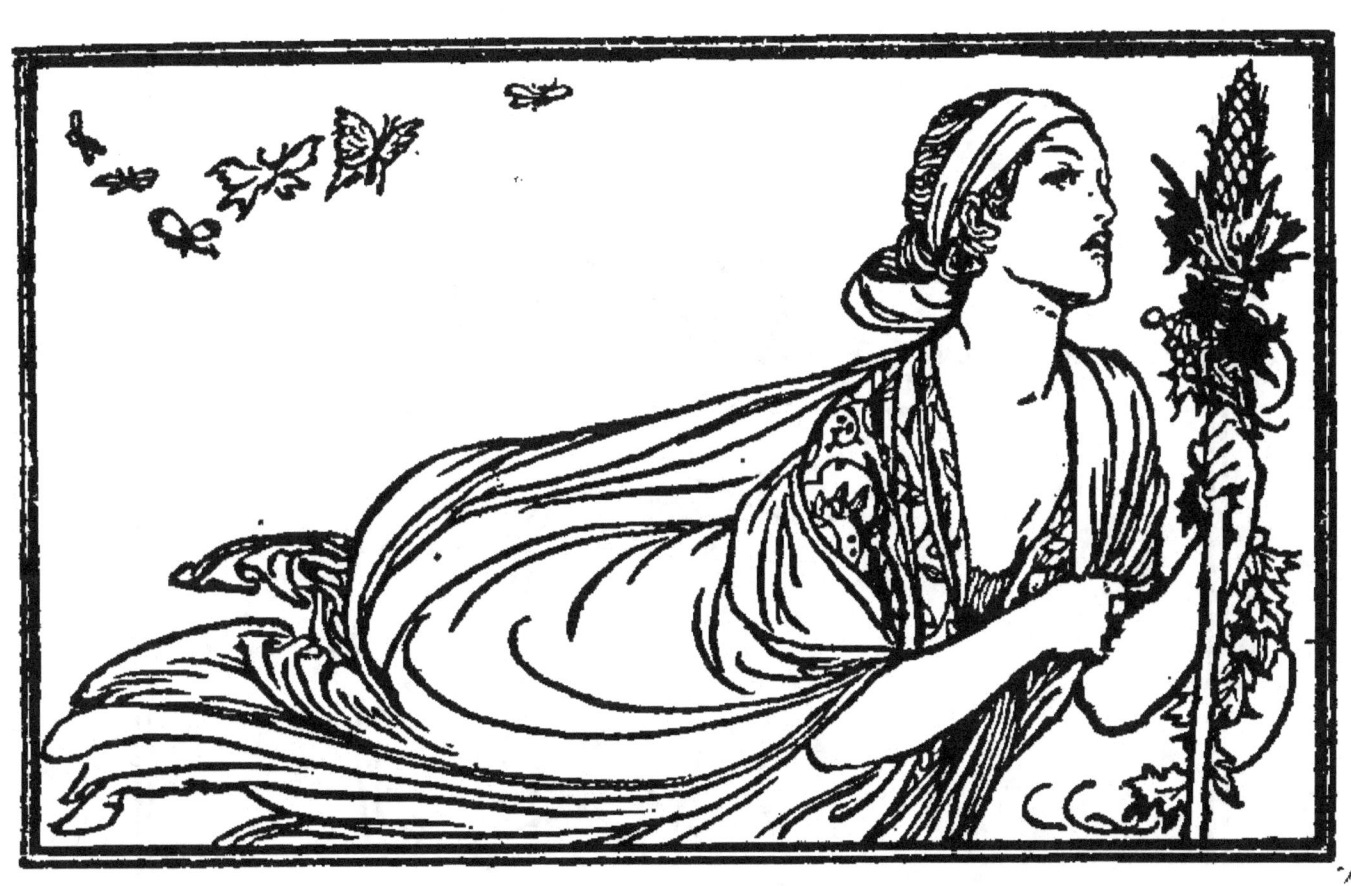

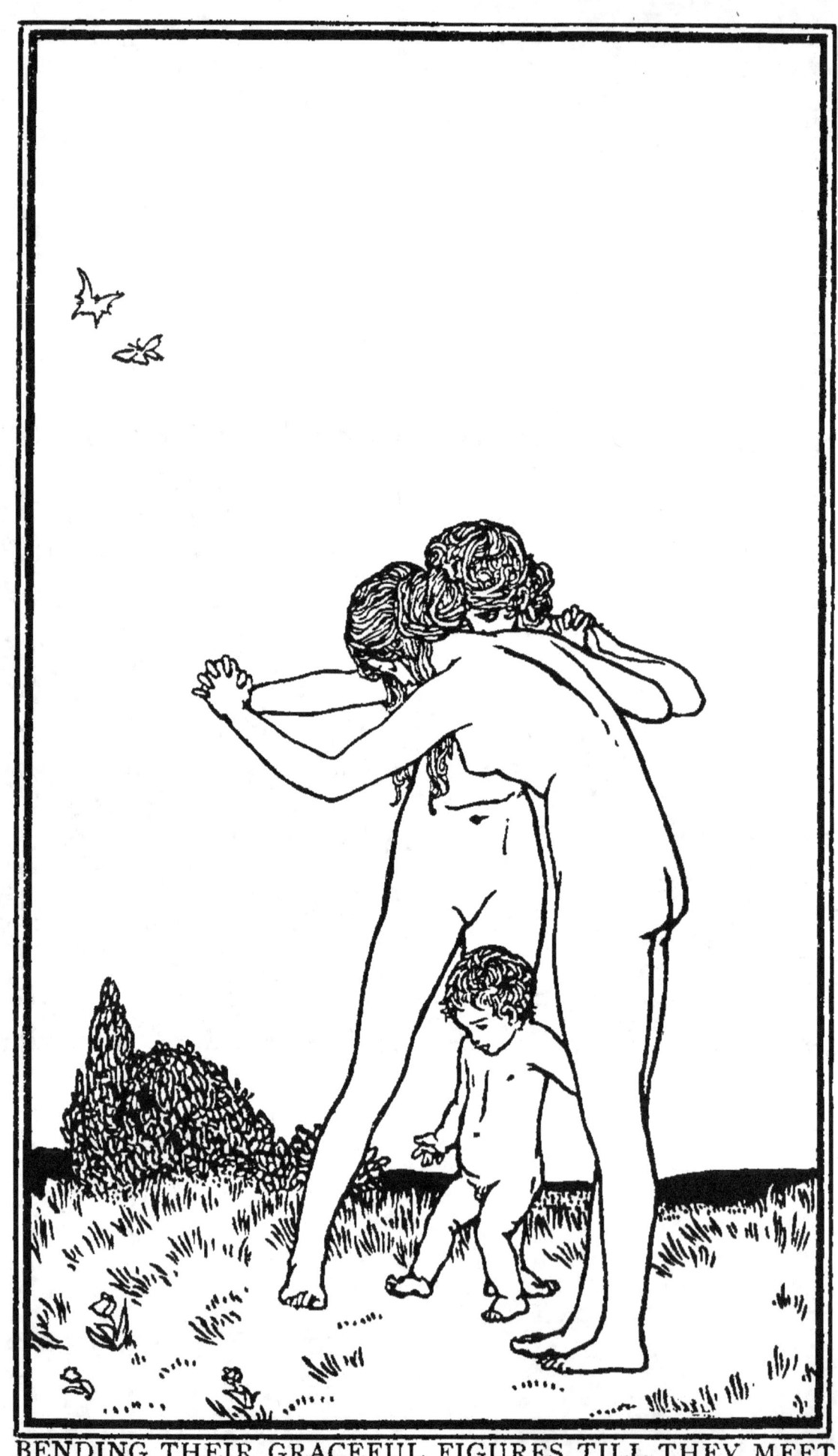

BENDING THEIR GRACEFUL FIGURES TILL THEY MEET OVER THE TRIPPINGS OF A LITTLE CHILD

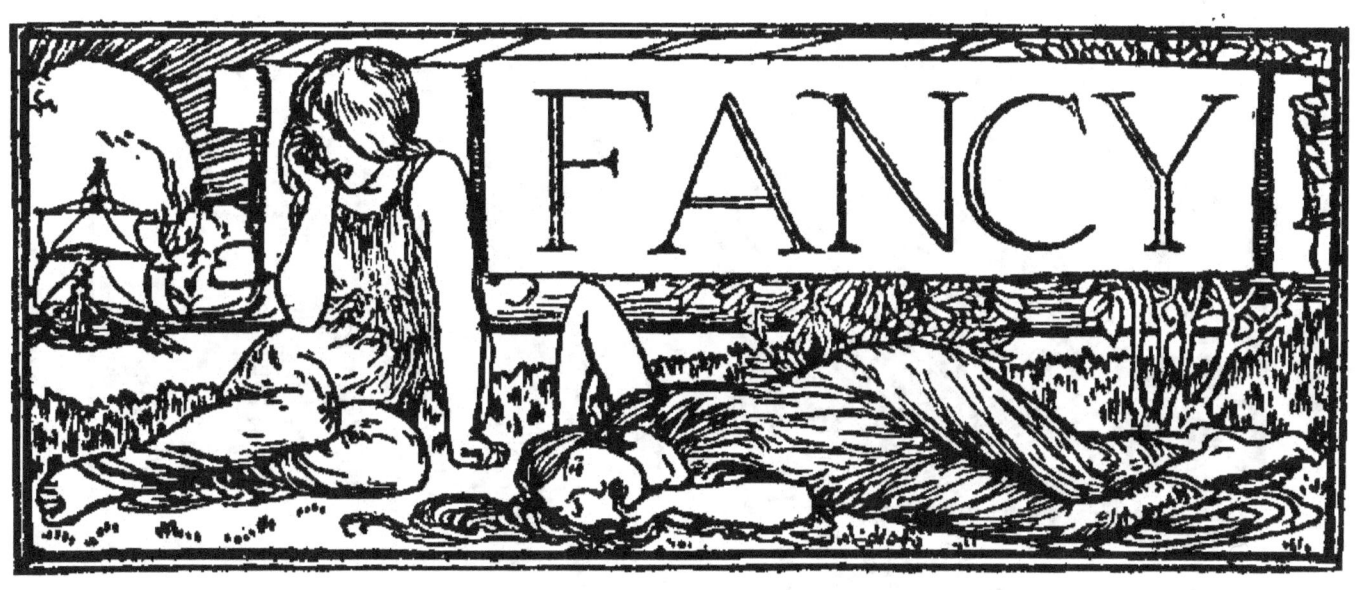

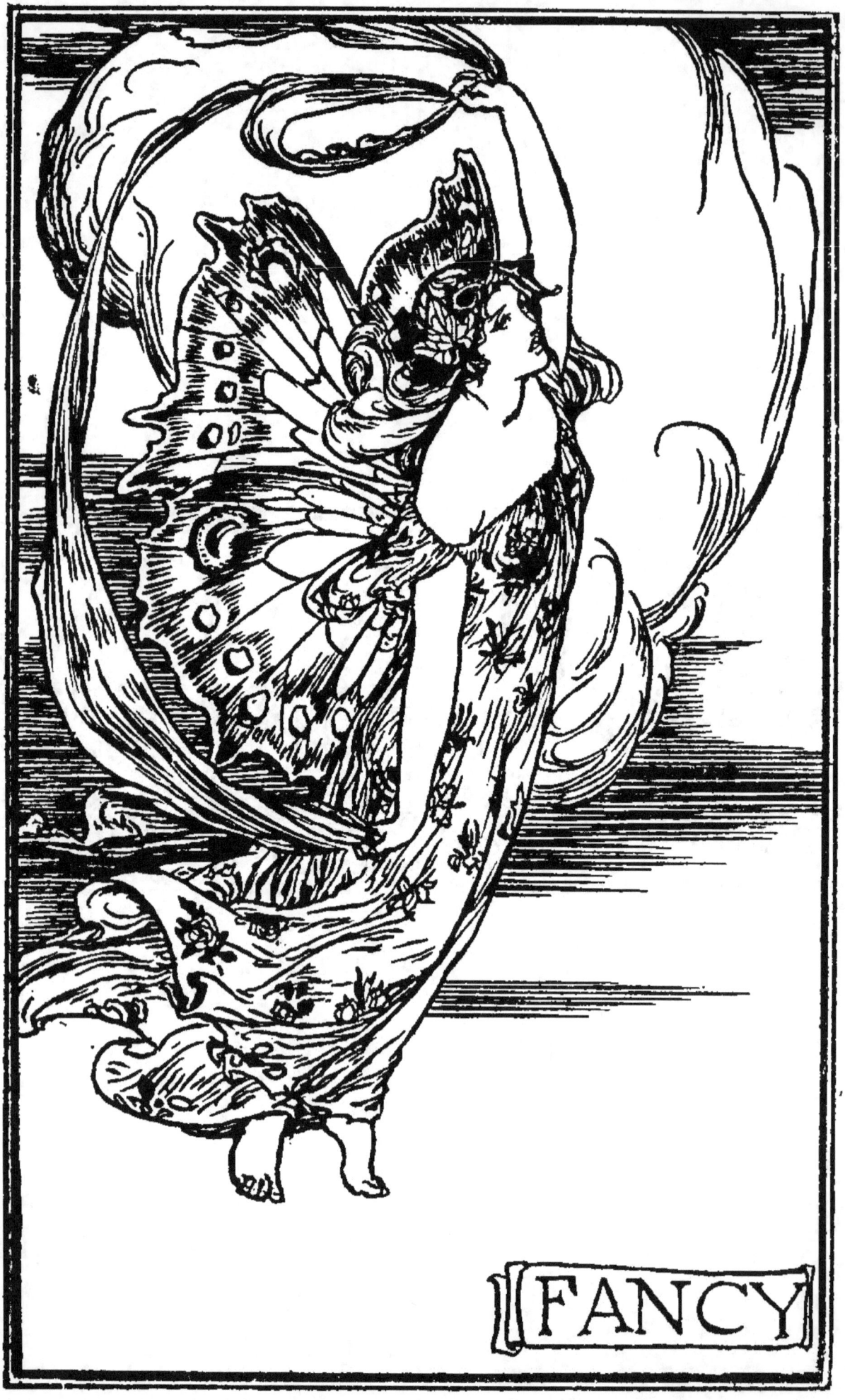

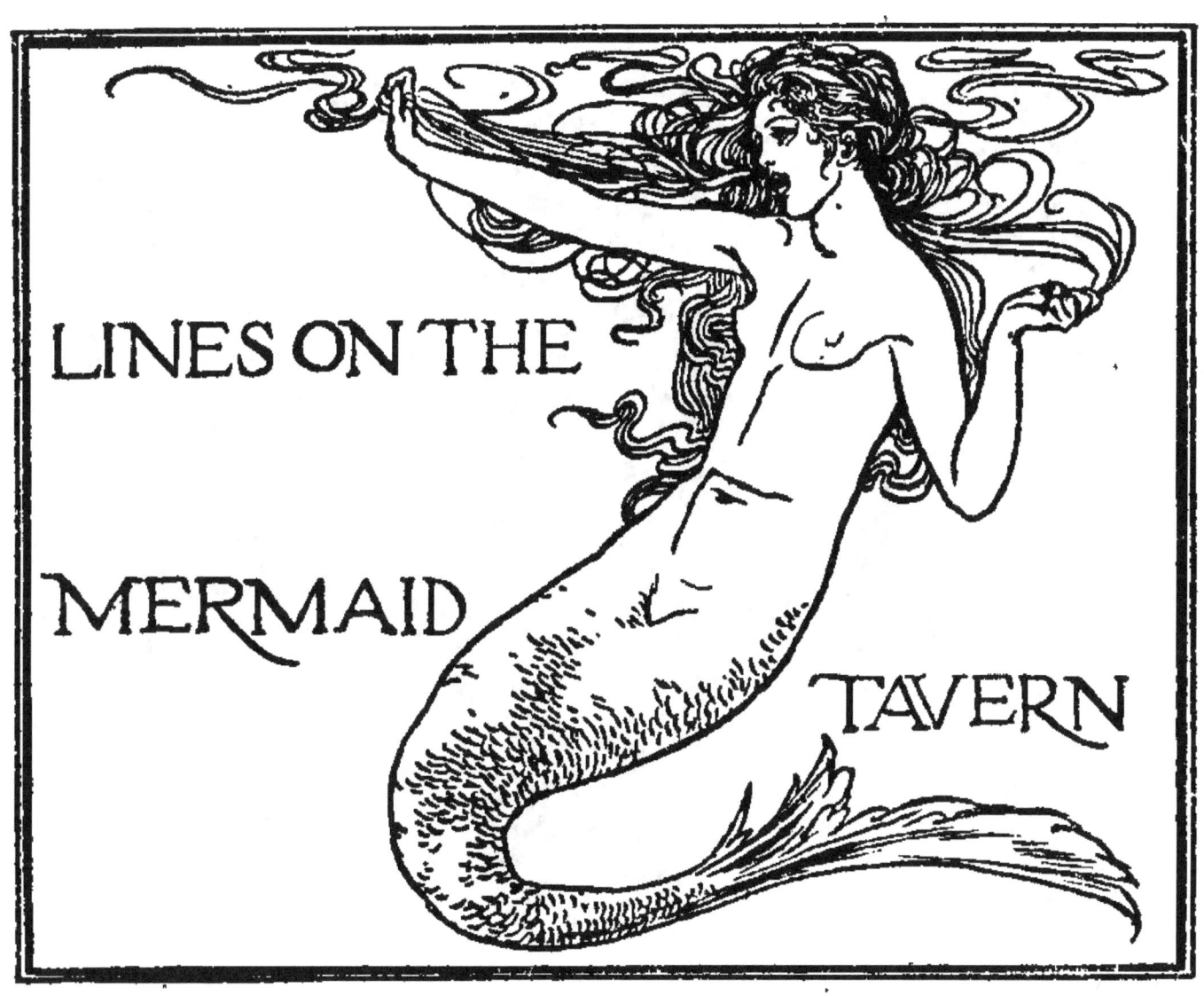

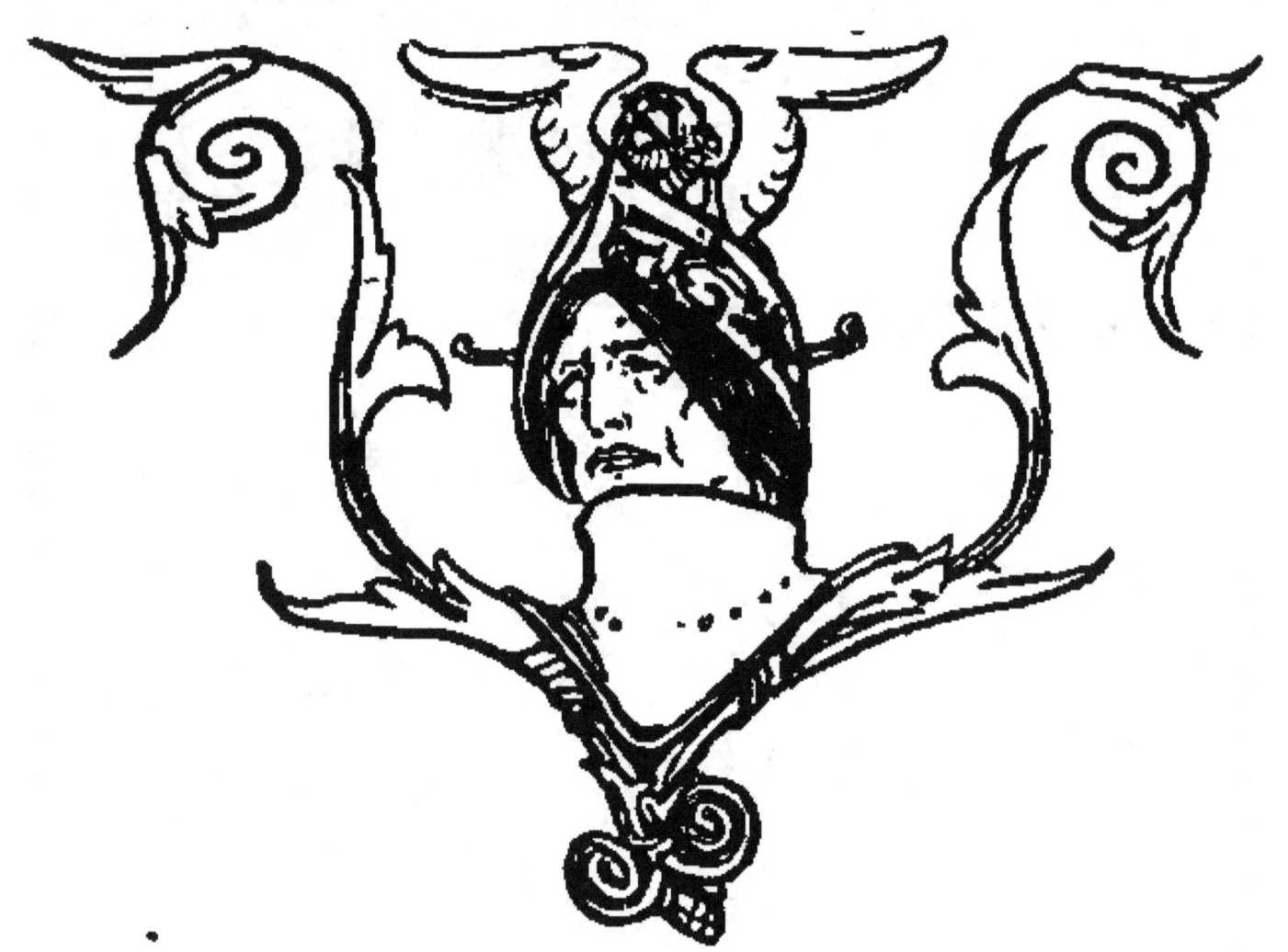

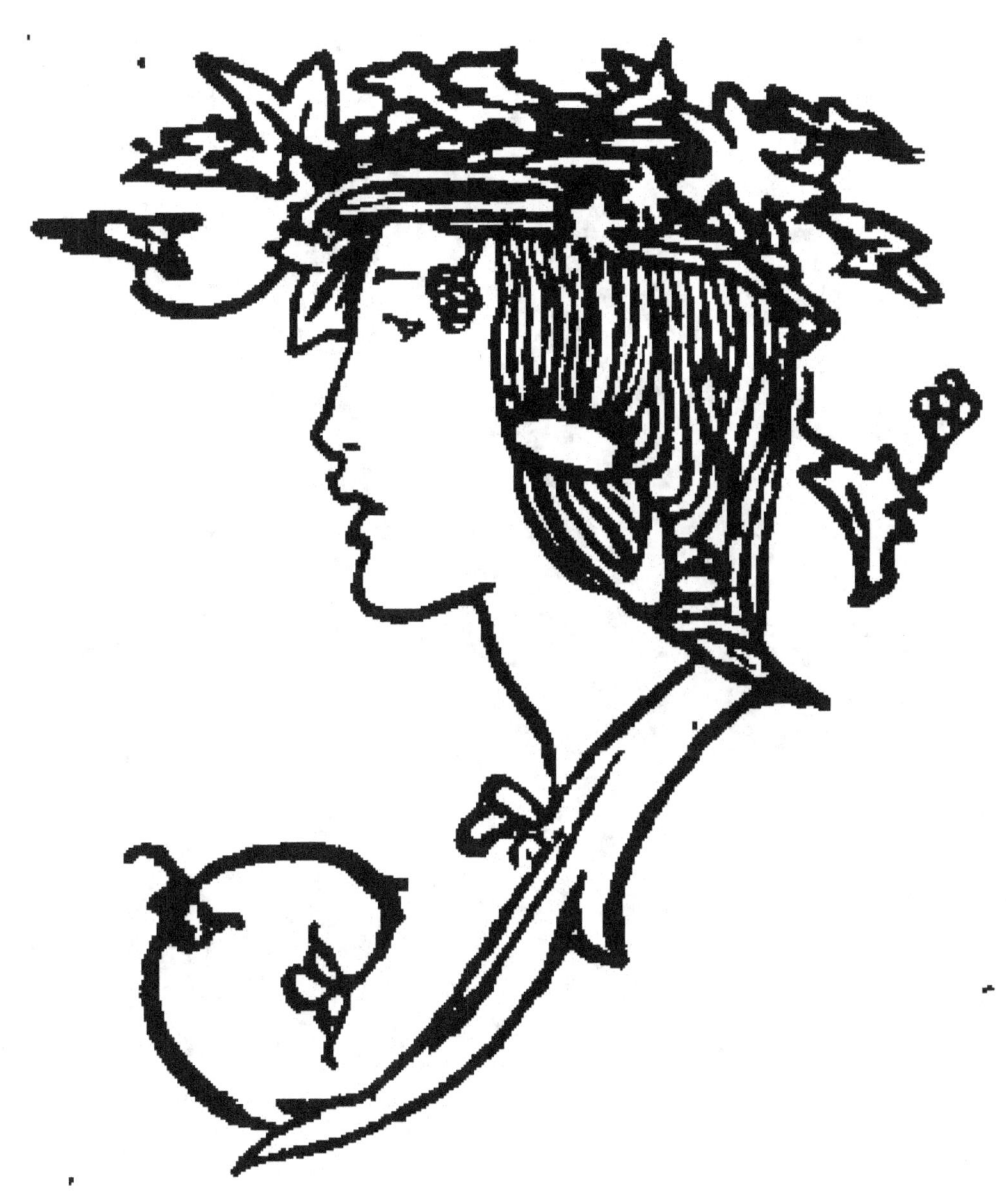

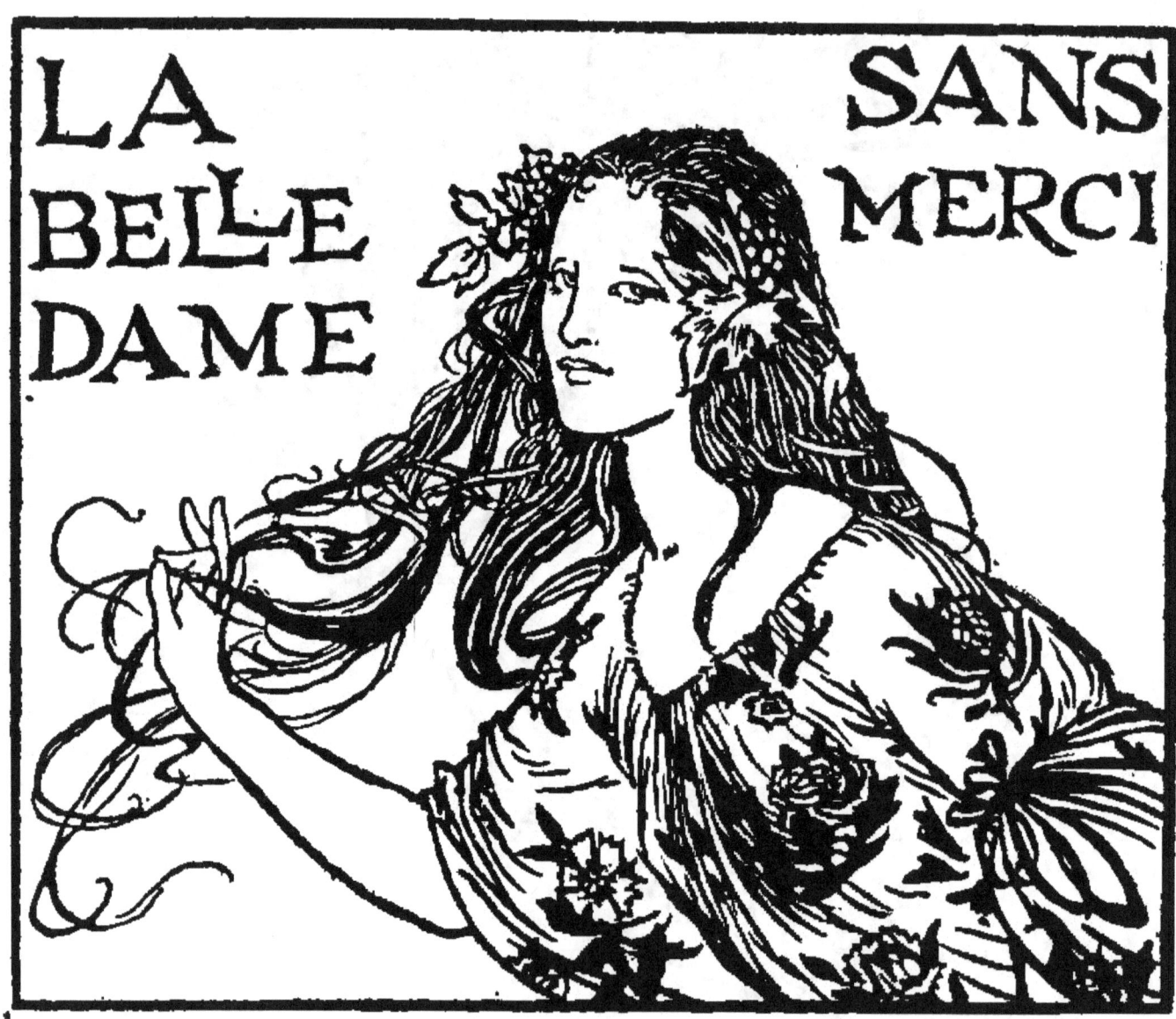

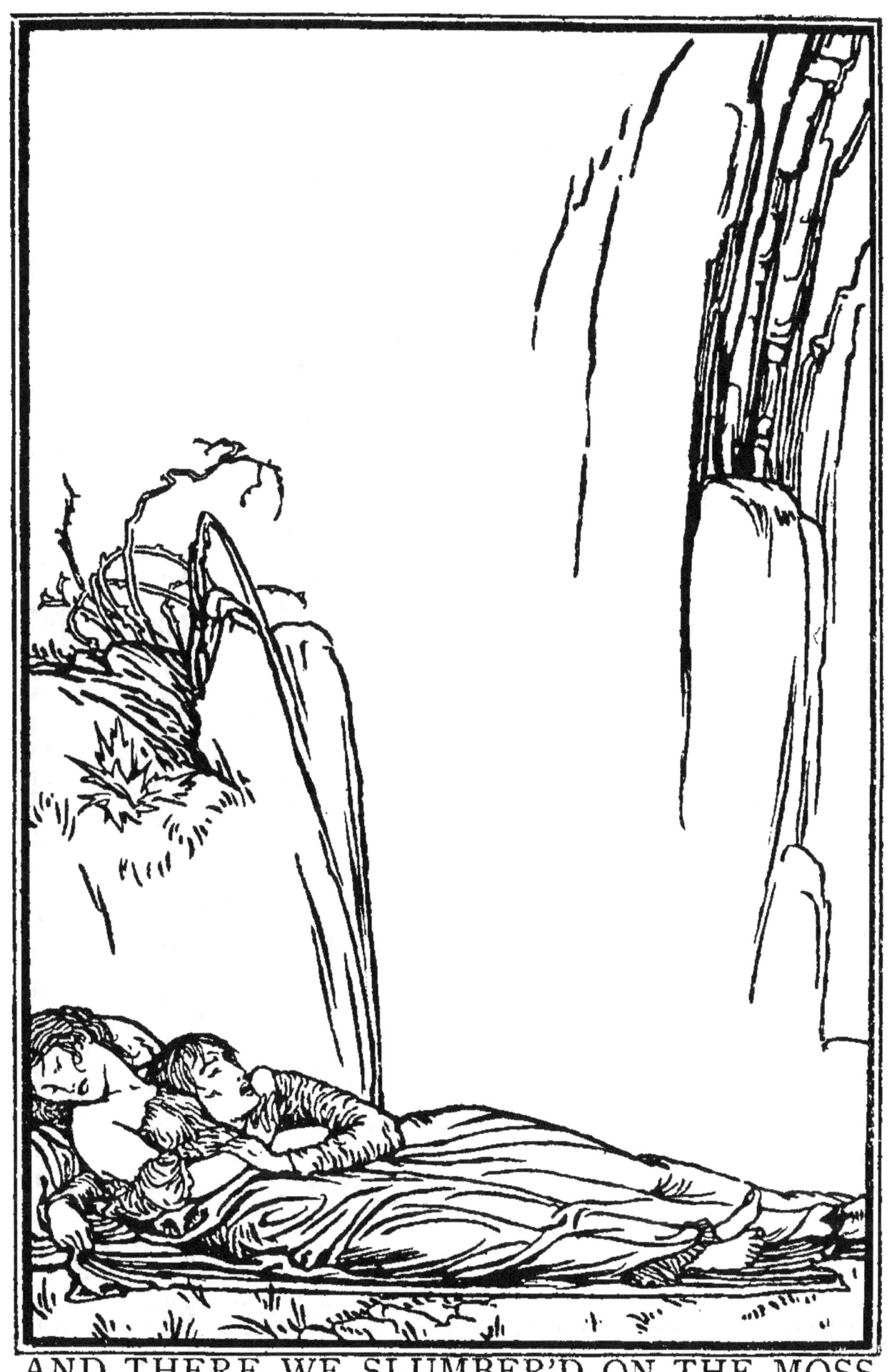

AND THERE WE SLUMBER'D ON THE MOSS
AND THERE I DREAM'D

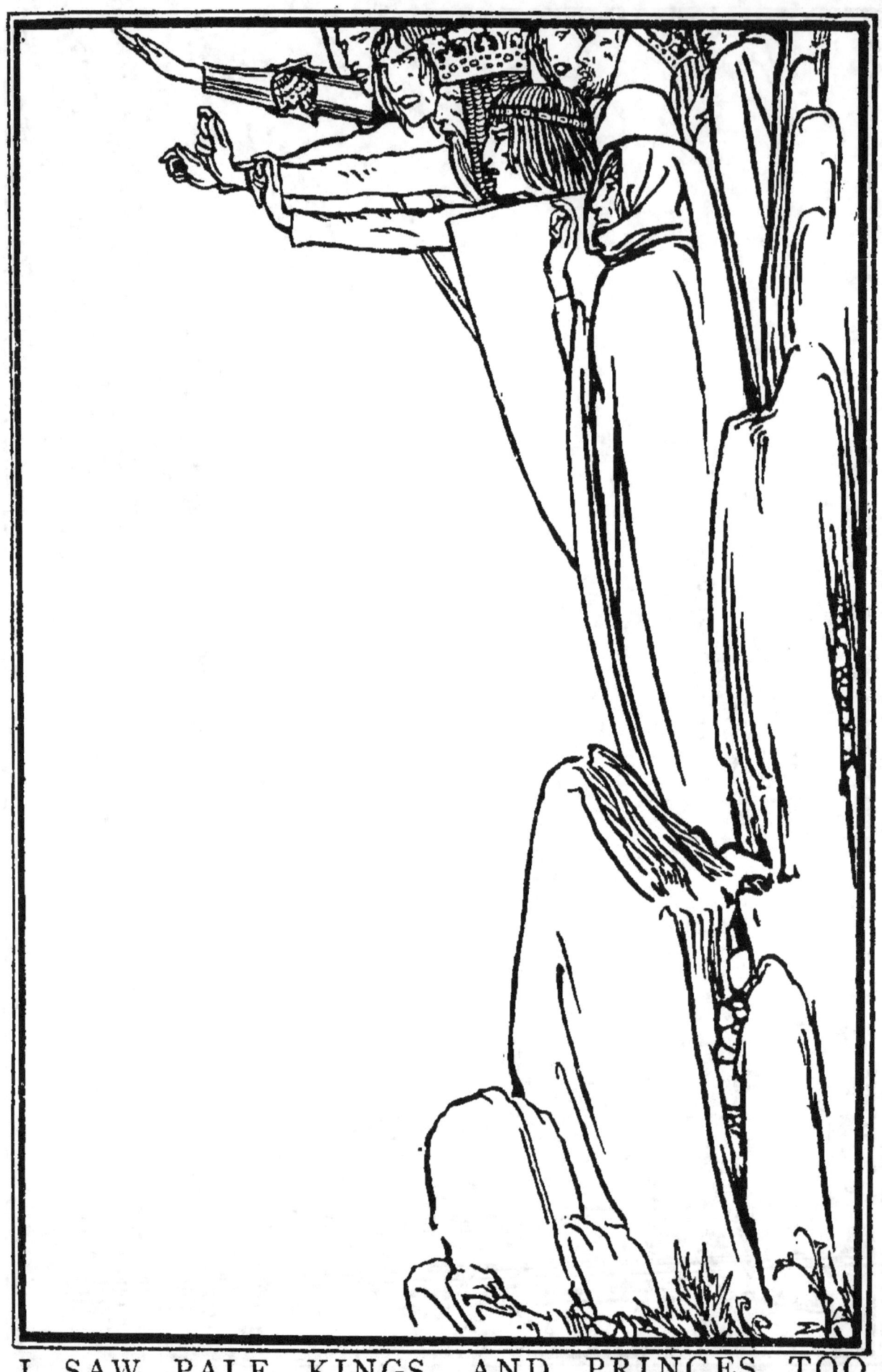

I SAW PALE KINGS, AND PRINCES TOO
PALE WARRIERS, DEATH-PALE WERE THEY ALL

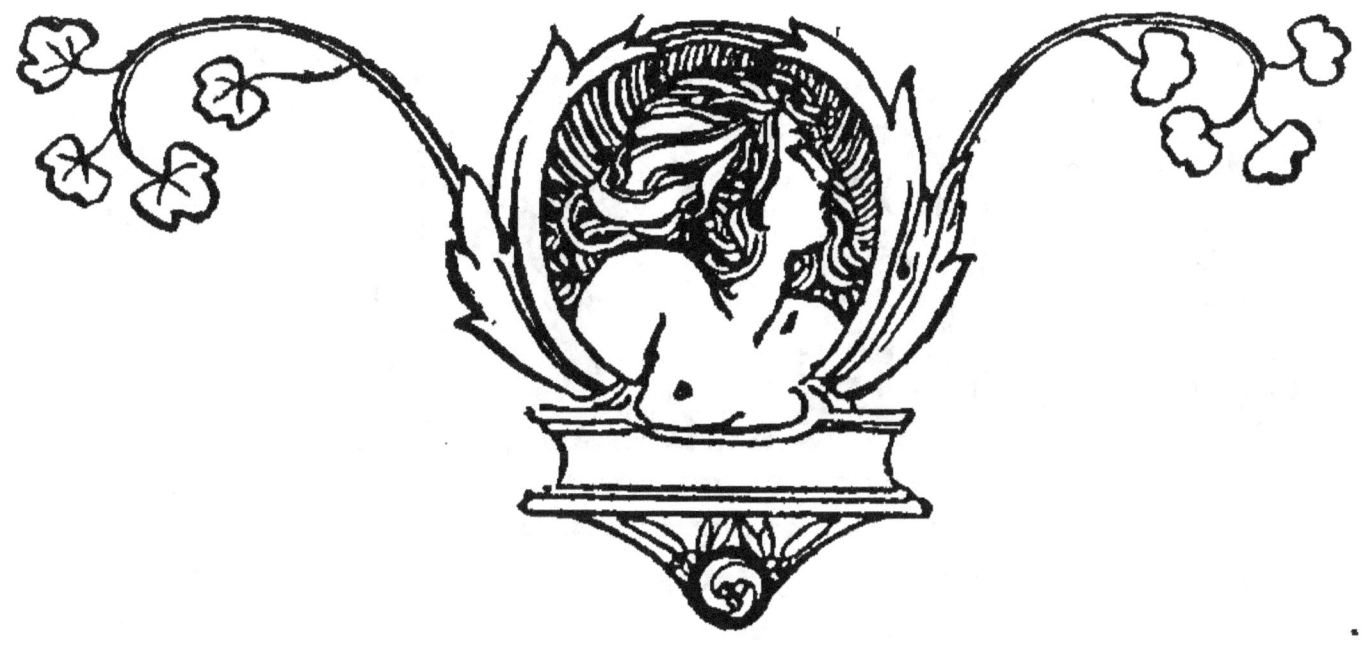

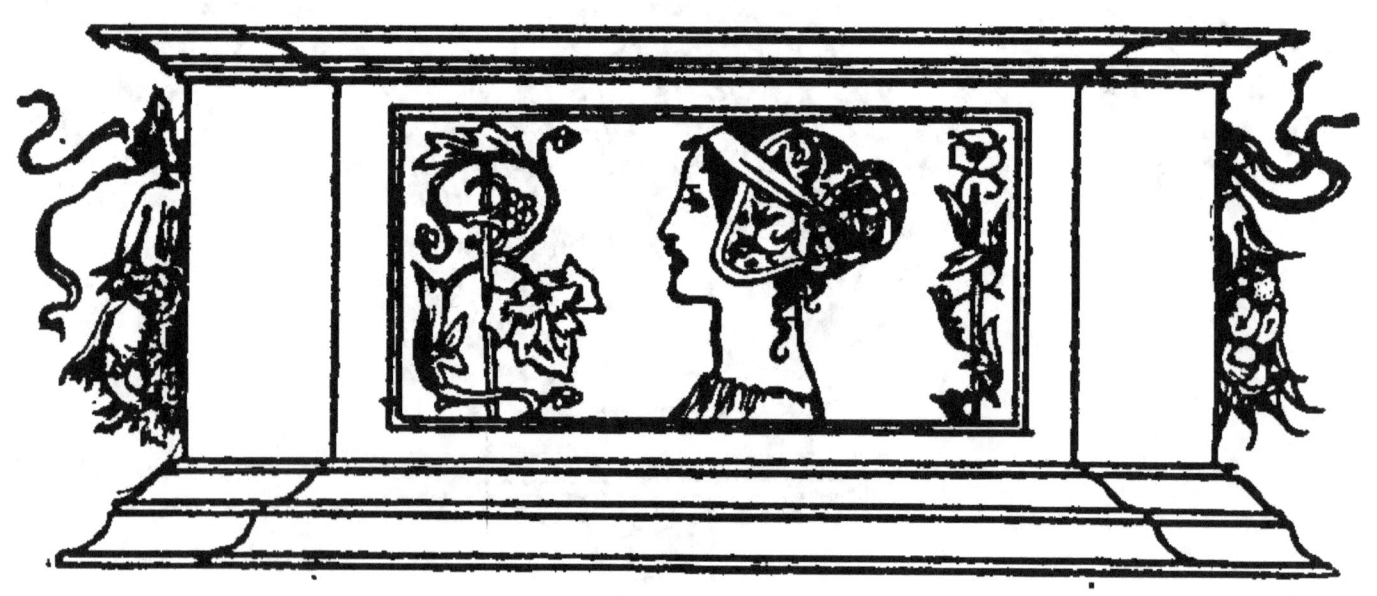

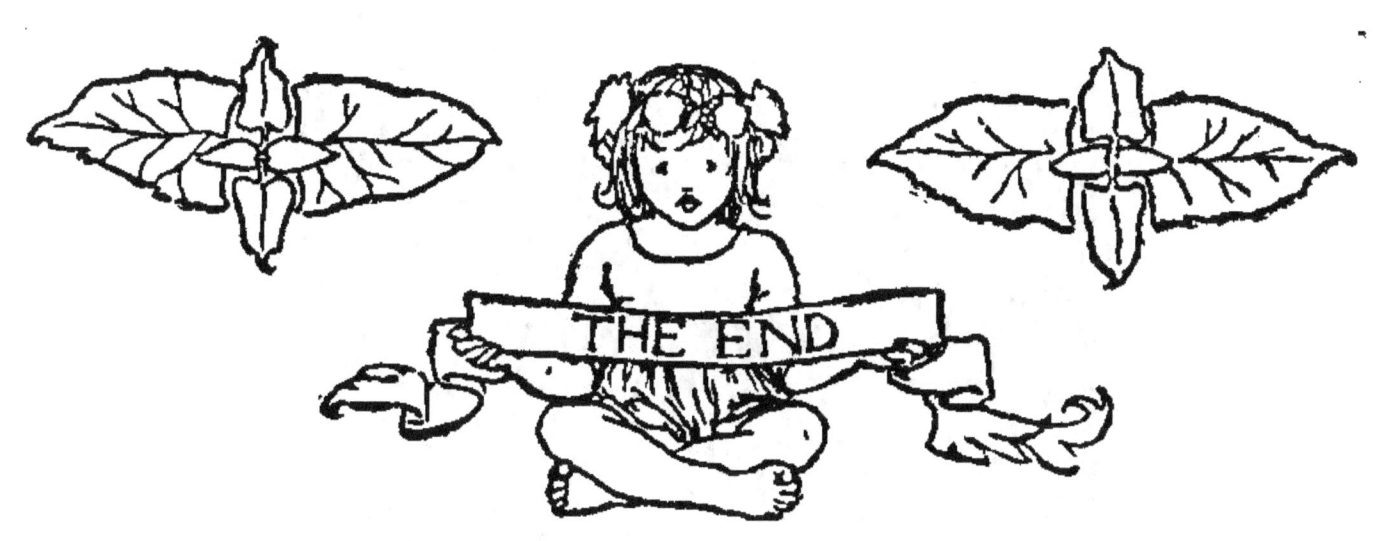

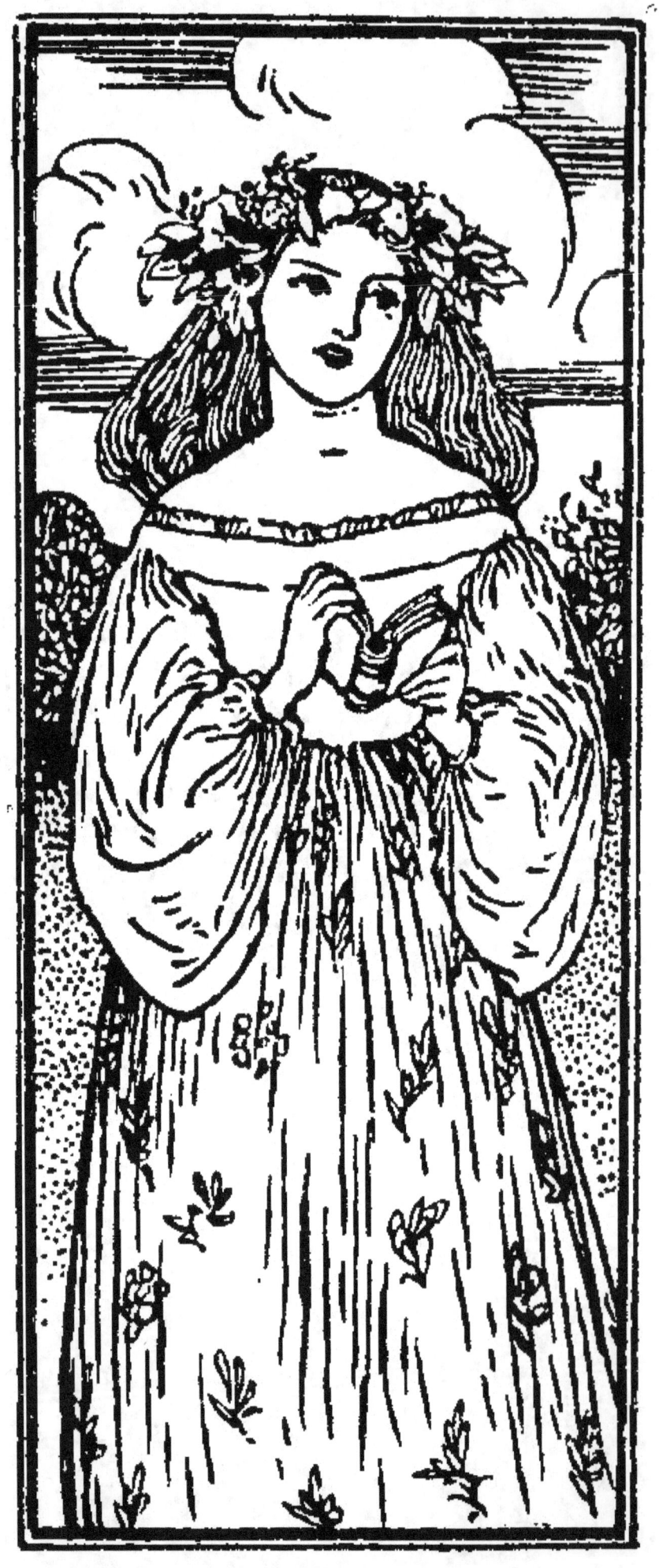

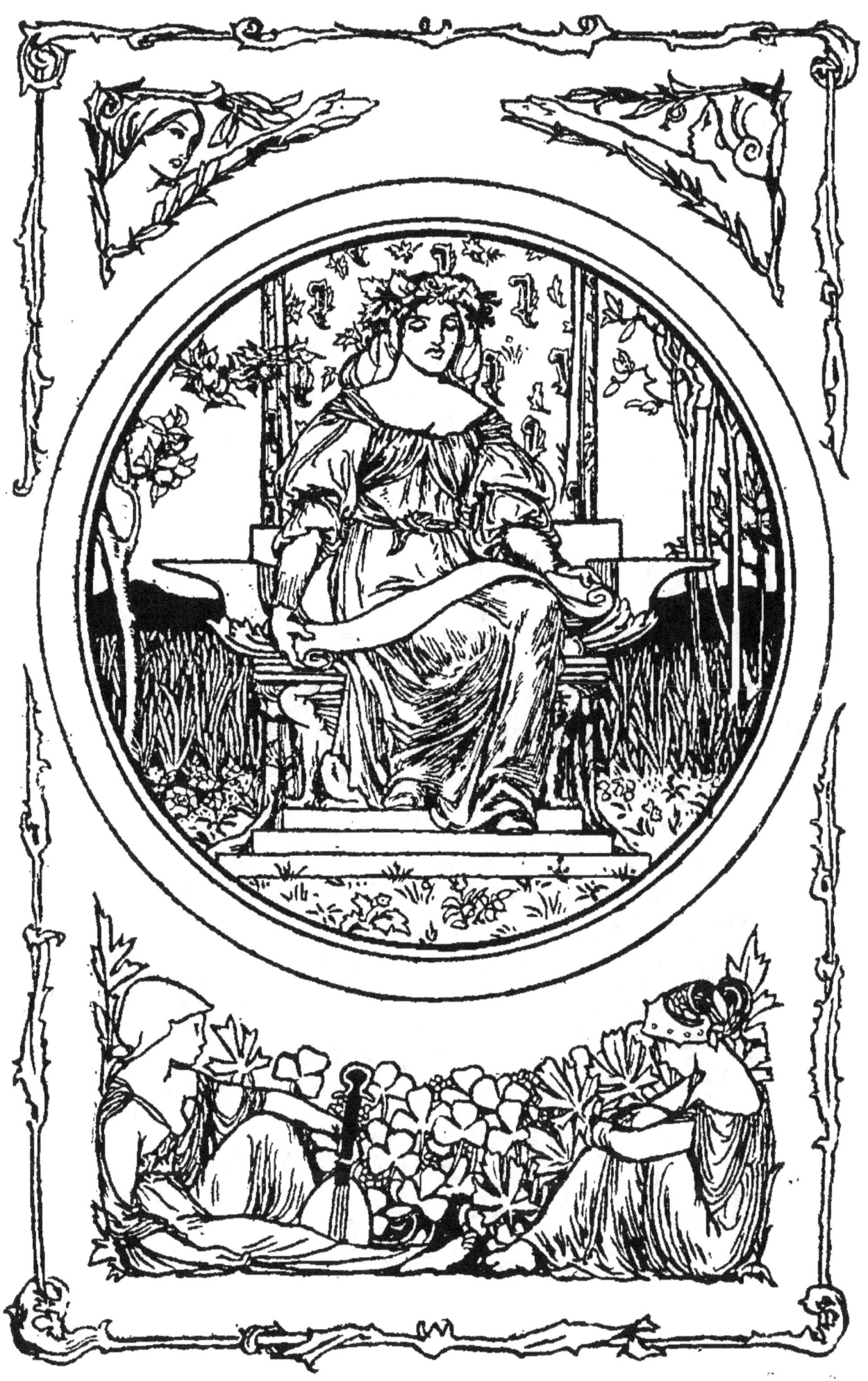

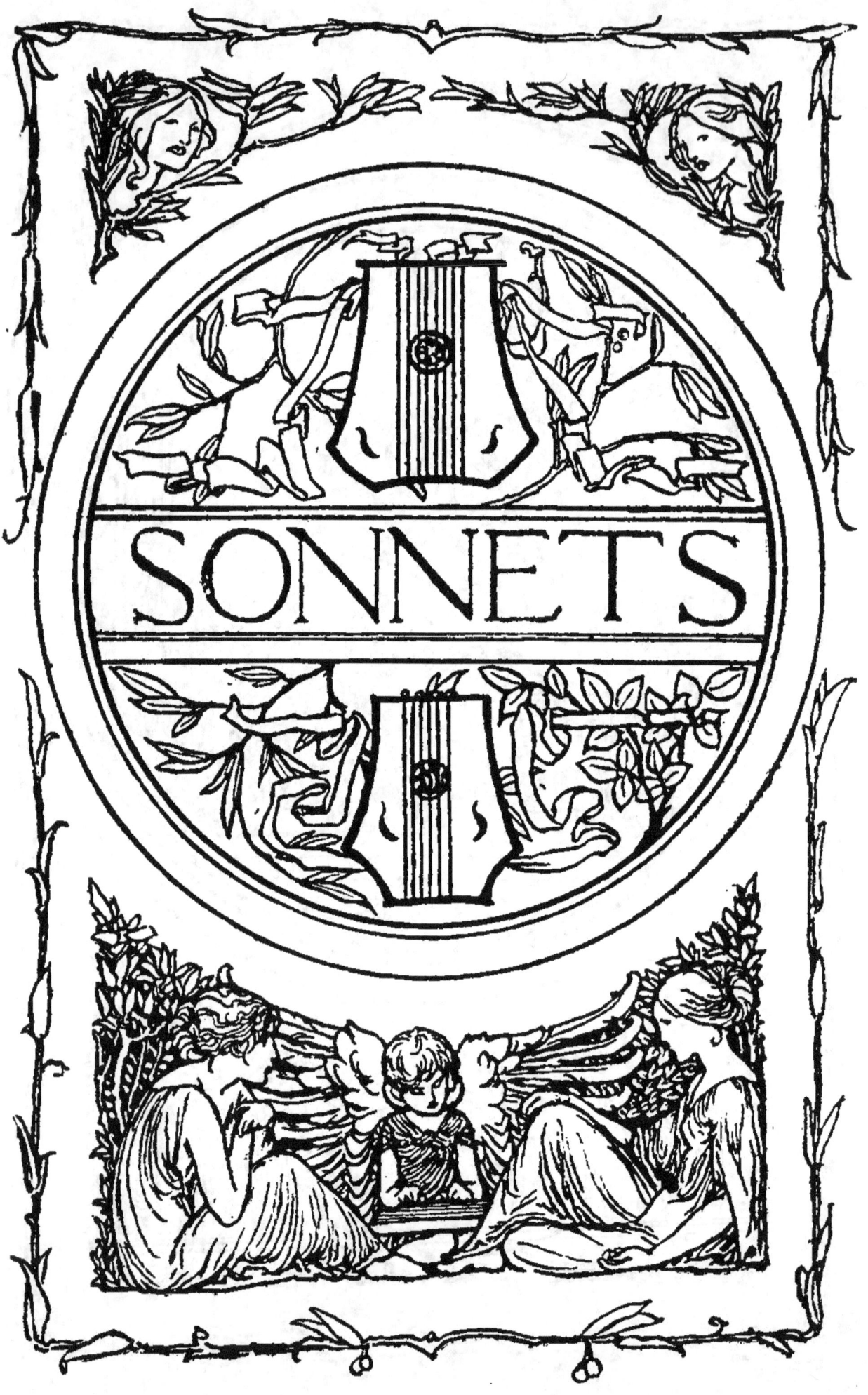

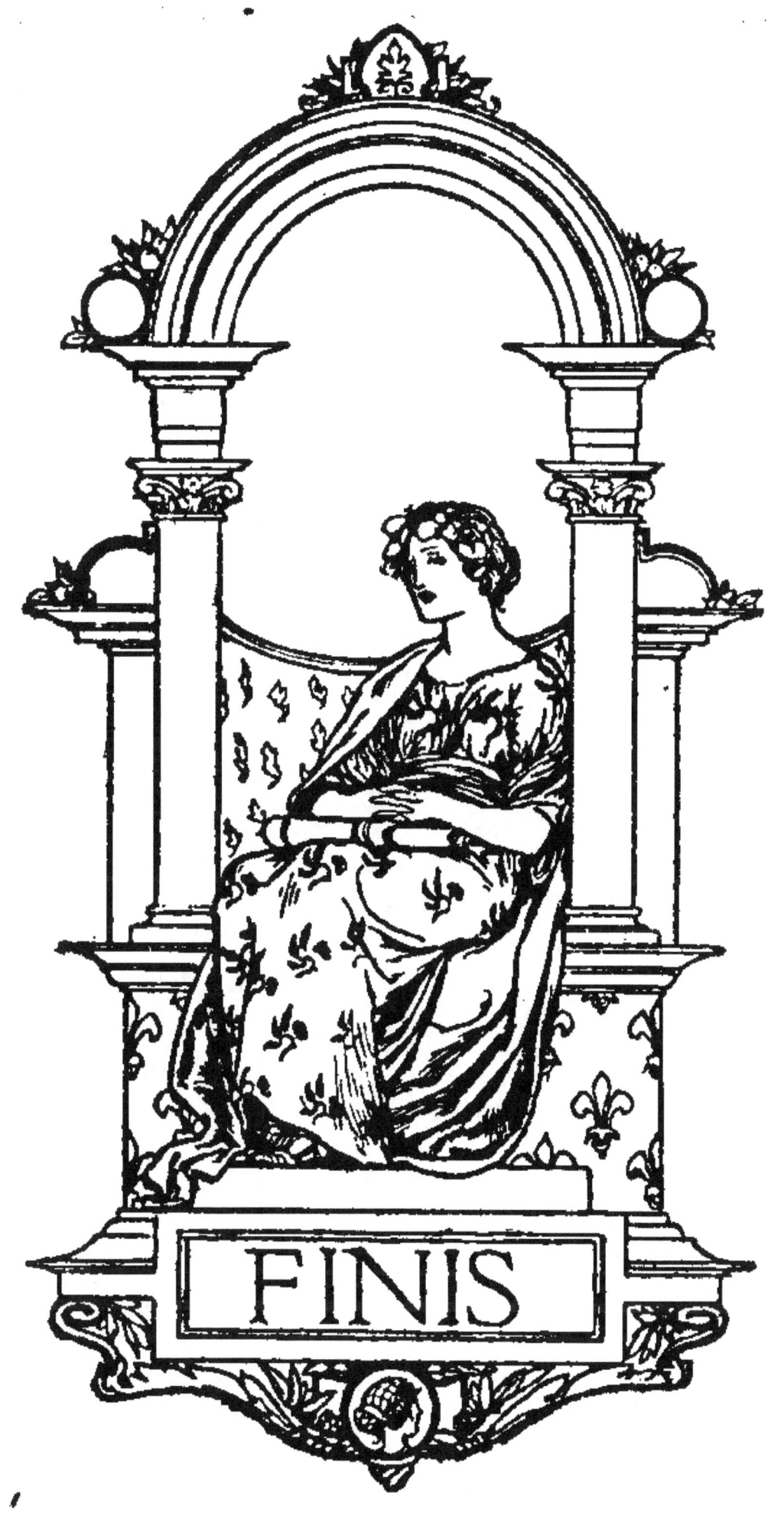